"Daniella offers important insight and suggestions on the very important element of risk taking."

—Wayne Berson, CEO, BDO USA, LLP

"*Ready, Set...Risk!* raises a number of important issues for both women striving to make the most of their careers, and for organizations like ours, that want to attract and retain female talent."

—Trisha Conley, Head of Talent & Resourcing,
Downstream, BP

"Daniella has compiled a diverse and distinct set of experiences and views as she helps the reader assess perspectives in risk."

—Connie Lindsey, Executive Vice President,
Head of Corporate Social Responsibility and Global
Diversity and Inclusion, Northern Trust

"Every time a woman chooses security and the safe bet over something new, she is missing the opportunity to achieve greater success and fulfillment in work and in life. *Ready, Set...RISK!* is filled with real-life stories that are engaging and inspiring....a very practical guide to developing the confidence and the ability to take calculated risks that lead to great reward."

— Debbie Storey, Senior Vice President,
Talent Development and
Chief Diversity Officer, AT&T

D1166302

Daniella T. Levitt

Ready, Set...RISK!

Brick Tower Press
Habent Sua Fata Libelli

Brick Tower Press
Manhanset House
Dering Harbor, New York 11965-0342
Tel: 212-427-7139
bricktower@aol.com • www.BrickTowerPress.com

Library of Congress Cataloging-in-Publication Data
Levitt, Daniella T.
Ready, Set...Risk! Positive Strategies and Tactics for Women to Turn Career Risk into
Opportunity.

ISBN 978-1-899694-01-3

1. Business & Economics, Careers-General 2. Business & Economics,
Entrepreneurship 3. Business & Economics, Personal Success 4. Business &
Economics, Women in Business

First Trade Paper Printing, May 2015

Daniella T. Levitt

Ready, Set...RISK!

Positive Strategies and Tactics for Women
to Turn Career Risk into Opportunity

"Only those who will risk going too far can possibly
find out how far one can go."
—T. S. Eliot

ACKNOWLEDGMENTS

As I was working with my publisher to prepare this manuscript for proof reading and final edits, he sent me a version of the document which included a blank page with just one word on it: "Acknowledgements." It was a not-so-subtle reminder that I still needed to get that done. It wasn't that I didn't want to write my "Acknowledgements" page; rather that I found the prospect of writing it more daunting than writing the actual book. After all, how does one possibly find an appropriate way to recognize all those people who in some way or another contributed to this book going from concept to reality? I guess by following my own advice—"starting somewhere and starting now," and hoping that in the process everyone who had anything to do with the book hears this message loud and clear from the bottom of my heart, "Thank you. I couldn't have done it without you."

My parents are my lifelong cheerleaders. You have always been there rooting for me in the stands, applauding my efforts, and encouraging me to have new and exciting experiences, even when it meant I chose to live half a world away from you. I can never thank you enough for everything you provided me with as a child that contributed to me becoming the *Ready, Set...RISK!* taker that I am. My husband Steve is my biggest supporter. Steve—I am so happy I took a risk and emailed you via the online dating site in 2004. You back me up as I pursue my ideas, you encourage me to keep pushing the boundaries, you cheer me up when I've had a tough day, you patiently turned down the volume on the TV when I was writing, and you let me take over the breakfast table for months for my writing spot. Thank you for all your love for me and belief in me.

I have many longstanding friends, colleagues and clients whom I told that I was going to write this book, who helped me bring it to fruition. There are many people that I have met throughout the process of writing the book that contributed in such meaningful ways to the end product. Some of you were a sounding board, some of you ended up being interviewees, some of you helped connect me to others in your network for interviews, and all of you provided nonstop encouragement. I am extremely grateful for your time and your support. I could not have done this without you.

Jamie Constantine—I am glad that I reached out my hand to say "Hello" and introduce myself as you were leaving the Board meeting at which we were both present. It marked the beginning of a wonderful friendship. Jamie in turn introduced me to Alan Morell, who is my agent. Alan—I am delighted that in the first twenty minutes of our very first meeting you grasped the scale of my vision, aspirations, and goals, and that you wanted me to be one of your clients. John Colby is my publisher. John—thank you for seeing the possibilities and potential in *Ready, Set...RISK!* when Alan presented you with my book proposal.

Last, but not least, I have two small furry friends (Porsche and Lotus), who kept me company nonstop while I wrote the book. In the early hours of the morning and throughout the day—day after day—our two cats sat next to me, or on my lap, or in the chair across from me, and kept me company. Writing a book is indeed a labor of love and it can get lonely at times. Not for me. While Porsche and Lotus will never be able to read these words, any of you reading this that have ever had a pet and loved them knows the love, peace, and contentment that animals bring into your life. Thank you to all the animals out there that give human beings unconditional love and company as we pursue our dreams.

CONTENTS

PART ONE: *"Ready...*   7

Chapter 1: "Great Women at the Table"   9

Chapter 2: Start Somewhere, Start Now   19

Chapter 3: Stretching Yourself on Your Risk-taking Continuums 29

Chapter 4: An Important Conversation   43

PART TWO: *"Ready, Set..."*   57

Chapter 5: Believe in Yourself   59

Chapter 6: Know Yourself   69

Chapter 7: The Power of Your Story   83

Chapter 8: The Critical Skill of Envisioning   97

Chapter 9: Communication Is Key   109

Chapter 10: Your Role Diversification Strategy   121

Chapter 11: Preparing for Your New Role   137

Chapter 12: Perspectives on Resilience and Power   149

Chapter 13: The Joy of Rescuing Yourself and Celebrating Yourself   161

PART THREE: *"Ready, Set...RISK!"*   175

Chapter 14: A Framework for Your Individual Roadmap   177

Chapter 15: An Organizational Perspective

                    —Creating the New Normal   191

Chapter 16: Ready, Set...RISK!   207

"The question isn't who is going to let me;
it's who is going to stop me."
—Ayn Rand

PART ONE: *"Ready..."*

Chapter 1: "Great Women at the Table"

Every few months I organize an intimate women's networking dinner. I call them G-WATT dinners. Like kilowatts, megawatts, and gigawatts, we women shine with our power, potential, and passion for everything we do. The acronym stands for "Great Women at the Table." There are usually somewhere between twelve and twenty women at each dinner, ranging in age from twenties to fifties. At one of the dinners I asked the women if they would be willing to spend a few minutes filling out a quick informal survey of eight questions I had put together on the subject of risk taking. I got seventeen surveys back.

The first question I asked was, "As you look back over your personal and professional journey to date, are there risks you have encountered in the past that you have NOT taken, and that you regret not taking?" The majority of women in their forties and fifties circled "YES," whereas the majority of women in their twenties and thirties circled "NO." The women who have journeyed for longer indicated regret about not taking risks more so than those women who are earlier in their lives and careers.

I asked the women if they would like to take more risks, personally and professionally. I also asked if they believed that with a variety of more types of support they would take more risks, personally and professionally. Eighty-eight percent of the respondents indicated they *would like to take more risks personally*, and 82 percent noted they *would like to take more risks professionally*. Eighty-eight percent of the respondents said that *with a variety of more types of support they would take more risks personally*, and 100 percent said that *with a variety of more types of support they would take more risks professionally*.

The results of this informal mini-survey correspond with the essence of what has surfaced in hundreds of conversations I have had on this topic of women and risk taking over the last couple of years—

particularly with regard to risk taking in the context of our careers. I have been exploring the extent to which we do or do not take calculated risks in our careers, how we feel about increasing our calculated risk taking in our careers, what kind of support we look for in our risk taking, and how we can prepare for our risk taking to increase our likelihood of success. Fundamentally, women approach decision-making and risk taking in their professional lives differently than men do. Women would like to increase their propensity for risk taking in their careers, increase their preparedness for risk taking, and increase their likelihood of success in their risk taking.

Do women actually take professional risks less often than men? The general perception is "yes." Almost everyone I speak with believes that women have a different propensity and appetite for risk than men do. In general the perception is that we take career-related risks less frequently than men. We can all summon up images right now of women we know who are glorious, wonderful, inspiring risk takers. But we can also all summon up images of exponentially more women we know who, for one reason or another, have not taken more risks in their career journey. We can all picture the many women whom we have heard say something along the lines of, "I wish I could have/would have taken that chance."

It makes me sad that more women don't take calculated risks more frequently in their careers, because it has repercussions for us on many fronts—both personally and professionally. It hurts us in our wealth and our health. It hurts us in what we end up with during negotiations. It hurts us in how we are represented in management, executive, and leadership ranks. If we as women want to drive more change on those fronts, we have to be comfortable with taking calculated risks in our careers more often. We have to enable ourselves to establish different strategies to successfully manage through risk encounters—strategies that are dependent not only on our own actions but also on the actions of others. We have to learn the language of risk. By learning the language of risk and applying it to ourselves, we are empowering ourselves to make different choices, and we are empowering ourselves to turn risk into opportunity by establishing different strategies for managing those risk encounters. Speaking the language of risk means we will enjoy the power and ability to shape our own destinies—more so than ever before.

From when I was a teenager I always believed I was destined to do something big and impactful, something that could fundamentally transform the lives of others. Over the last two years I recognized that this was it. I could positively impact women in their professional risk-taking propensity, preparedness, and likelihood of success with their risk taking. As I looked back over the course of my life and my career, I recognized the array of significant risks that I had taken, both professionally and personally, what had motivated me to take them, how I had planned for them and managed my way through them, the results, and the course my life had taken as a consequence. I listened to the women who heard my story and who responded with, "Wow... I wish I could take those kinds of risks too." I played back in my head my response to them, which was invariably, "You can! You too can turn risk into opportunity!" Yet as I looked around I realized that there was a distinct lack of good, substantive material and support out there to aid women in risk taking in their careers. I am on a mission to change that. This book will now change the conversation when it comes to women taking risks and turning them into opportunity in their careers.

This book equips women everywhere, of all ages, with concepts, tools, and courage—concepts to help you challenge your current thinking, to realize there are no limitations to what you can accomplish, and to shift how you and others see your risk-taking appetite and abilities. Tools to help you to reframe risks into opportunities so that you will pursue them with intention, passion, and joy, and to establish new strategies and techniques to successfully navigate the risky course you have chosen. Courage to take risks you might not have taken before. Women don't live and work in isolation. Our desire and ability to be successful in taking more risks and turning them into opportunities in our careers is significantly impacted by leadership in the organizations in which we work. This book will also now change the conversation amongst organization's leaders, helping them to develop strategies and plans to support women in their risk taking. Research has shown that better business results are achieved by having more women in leadership. There is a seed change that has to happen in the culture and fabric of an organization that embraces supporting women in their risk taking as they aspire to move forward and upward. Concepts, tools, and courage—you need all three to be able to risk effectively and with confidence. I view myself as a serial risk taker, and I have always needed all three of those in every step of my journey.

I grew up in South Africa, living there until I was twenty-six. It's an incredibly beautiful country—I encourage you to go visit. But it is also a country marred by political turmoil. I grew up during the seventies and eighties, when apartheid was rampant and tearing the country apart. In retrospect, I truly believe that is where my fascination with transformational change began. I was living through change, seeing firsthand the impact apartheid had on individuals, families, businesses, and the country as a whole. From the institution of apartheid, to the Soweto Riots, to our maid who lived with us instead of with her own family, to bombs going off in downtown Johannesburg, to the freeing of Nelson Mandela, to the recognition of the ANC as a legitimate political party and the first truly democratic elections that ushered in Nelson Mandela as President—that's transformational change. South Africa is and always will be a core part of who I am.

South Africa inspired my lifelong career journey focusing on transformational change at a macrolevel with organizations and at a microlevel with individuals. South Africa taught me that without significant risk there is no significant change for oneself or for others. South Africa taught me that the road to transformation is fraught with risk and uncertainty, but if you have a powerful vision that is a fundamental truth, and if you can successfully craft, communicate, and engage others in that shared vision and truth, then others will travel that road with you. South Africa taught me that it can be a long road to success, but when you fail in your first attempt to accomplish your objective, you pick yourself up, you regroup, you adapt your strategy, and you keep moving forward towards the endgame. South Africa taught me that differences in people matter in a wonderful way, and that both the greatest risks and the greatest rewards come from embracing those differences. These lessons and many others have served me well in my journey of serial risk taking.

My risk taking started early. Even as a teenager I wanted to experience the world. Immediately after high school—instead of following the conservative and traditional path of going straight to university—I took a personal risk and spent the better part of a year doing an international program at the Hebrew University in Jerusalem with other similar-minded students from all around the world. Severely bitten by the global exposure bug, upon my return to South Africa I immediately secured a waitressing job to fund my international trips throughout my university years. By the time I achieved my postgraduate degree at twenty-three years of age, I had seen more of the world than almost anyone else in my high school graduating class—all paid for out of my own savings—and I had also validated my desire to come and live in the United States of America, ideally in Chicago.

My risk taking has perpetuated my professional career. For my postgraduate studies I attended the Business School at the University of the Witwatersrand in Johannesburg. Part of the program was a three-month internship. Knowing my end goal was to be employed by a global consulting firm, with no qualms whatsoever I took my first professional risk and approached Andersen Consulting about doing the internship with them. I ended up being one of three interns they brought on, which subsequently turned into full-time job offers for all three of us upon graduation. My vision of moving to the United States came to fruition in 1996, when after three years of working for Andersen Consulting in Johannesburg, I started looking for opportunities in the United States. I was offered a job with Deloitte Consulting, with a home base in—of all places—Chicago! At twenty-six years old, with a job offer and H1-B visa in hand, I took my second professional and personal risk. I resigned from Andersen, packed my bags, and moved to the United States on my own to build a whole new life for myself. With a grand total of about $10,000 to my name, and ignoring a senior male partner at Andersen who made it a point to tell me repeatedly that I was too young to do this and would not make a success of myself by making this move, I did the only things

I knew how to do best—believe in myself, take a risk, and move forward.

My professional risk taking continued. I barreled along successfully in my career at Deloitte until, in 2007, in what came as a shock to many people, I took my biggest professional risk to date when I decided to walk away from Deloitte in the year that I was making my final run towards becoming a Partner. More about this later, but suffice it to say that after pursuing this goal wholeheartedly for so long, leaving was a huge risk, a huge decision, and not arrived at lightly. After spending eighteen months at Aon in what I quickly recognized was a transitional role (somewhat like the transitional boyfriend after breaking up a long-term relationship), in 2008 I left Aon and took my next major professional risk by founding my first company—Ovation Global Strategies, LLC. The company continues to go strong, working with corporations on complex, large-scale transformational change initiatives.

In 2013 I took yet another risk and launched a second business— this one focused primarily on development and advancement of women in the workplace. The differentiating pillars of the platform are working with individuals and corporations on risk taking and cross-generational collaboration as positive strategies to accelerate the pace at which women move forward and upward in their careers. I continue to risk as I design, develop, and conduct innovative and groundbreaking programs that have not been done before, that positively challenge and change the way corporations and individuals are approaching development and advancement of women in the workplace. As these concepts took on a life of their own I wrapped some of them under a separate umbrella—Daniella Levitt Enterprises, LLC. I know that doing what others have not yet tried to do is a risk. I know some of my risks will succeed gloriously and others will fail gloriously. But I am not afraid to try, and I am not afraid to risk.

I am not afraid to risk because, in keeping with my lessons from growing up in South Africa and the years since, I know how to drive complex, systemic, and sustainable transformational change. I know that we need significant change when it comes to development and advancement of women in the workplace. I know—and the research proves it out—that companies that embrace increasing representation of women in their leadership ranks show better business results. I know I have a powerful vision around risk taking and cross-generational collaboration that are fundamental truths. I know that as I successfully craft, communicate, and engage others in that shared vision and truth, others are beginning to travel that road with me. I know that it will be a long road to success; but I have had many successes and will continue to have more. Even when I do encounter a specific failure, I am resilient. I pick myself up, I regroup, I adapt my strategy, and I keep moving forward towards the endgame. I am also not afraid to risk, because I fundamentally believe in my concepts, I know how to make great use of the tools I have developed along the way, and I have a lot of courage that I am not afraid to draw on.

But this book is not about me. It's about you! It's about equipping you with concepts and tools, and empowering you to draw on your own courage—which indeed you have—so that you too can take calculated risks more often in your career and turn them into opportunity. I recognize that people have different tolerances for risk. I recognize that risk frames difficult issues and difficult choices. But as women we need to do a much better job of understanding, for each of us individually, where we fall on our own risk-taking continuums, why, and how we can shift our position. We need to learn the language of risk and how to apply it to ourselves so that we make different choices and turn more risks into opportunity, so that we shape our own destinies more so than ever before. The survey I did at dinner that night was clearly informal, but it was yet another affirmation of what I hear from women of all ages as I speak with them about taking risks in their careers. One: Women do want to increase their propensity for, preparedness for, and likelihood of success with their risk taking in their professional careers. Two: Women would be more willing to take those risks if they were provided with better support on both the professional front and the personal front during the course of their risk taking.

While there are certainly some nuances on dealing with career risk in the different generational groups, for the most part these perspectives are shared across the generations. So as women of all ages seek to lay claim to their destinies, it is imperative that women collaborate across the generations to help each other with their risk taking in their careers. Band together we should and we must, because we share in the fears and emotions that hold us back from taking more personal and professional risks. When I asked the women at dinner that night what those fears and emotions are, across all the age groups I heard words like failure, financial exposure, insecurity, job security, embarrassment, speaking up more, being in over one's head, demands on time and energy, and requiring more of oneself than one can commit to. I heard responses such as disappointment, protecting one's reputation, not making an impact that is broader than just oneself, anxiety, the unknown, losing one's personal and professional network. I heard concerns about lack of knowledge or competence, looking unintelligent, lack of confidence in being selected, and shattered confidence if not successful. The list continues, with responses such as not being authentic, and organizational cultures and environments that don't support vulnerability, authenticity, growth, and development of employees. The women were worried about uncertainty, letting people down, being unhappy, instability, appearing disloyal, starting over, what other people will say, lack of support from family and friends, and impact on family and friends.

Band together we should and we must, because we also share in what we have lost out on by not taking more risks. When I asked women that night what they believe they have lost out on by not taking more risks, across all the age groups I heard words and phrases like exposure to more interesting experiences and people and knowledge, independence, elevated satisfaction, career opportunities and career status, networking, and increased levels of personal satisfaction and happiness. They spoke about losing out on the following: branching out, stronger committed relationships, the exhilaration of the challenge, strength through knowing one can do it, more money, growth and change, professional advancement, change in profession, living in more countries, and starting more businesses. Other responses on what the women feel they have lost out on included being more assertive in challenging opinions of others, promoting one's own skills and championing oneself, challenging one's own capabilities, spending time on more fulfilling relationships, improving mental health, confidence, family time, and enjoying life.

I believe that luck and fate play a part in our lives and the journey each of us take; however, I do not believe in leaving things purely to luck and fate. We must hold ourselves accountable for leading a fulfilling and happy life. Our moments of greatest risk often provide our moments of greatest clarity and concentration, learning, and growth. Whether it is in a personal or professional situation, we all use our experience, emotions, and beliefs to attempt to determine the severity of the risk we face in any situation. Then we make our personal choices based on our individual interpretation of that situation, and we prepare ourselves accordingly. If we challenge our thinking and change our individual interpretation, if we change the choices we make and how we prepare to navigate through risk, we can arrive at a different set of outcomes. We can discover our full potential and become everything that each of us can be.

As you make use of the strategies and tactics in this book, you will look at risks in your career in a new light—in some cases by doing things you would not have considered at all in the past, in other cases by re-evaluating opportunities and the amount of risk associated with them, and in some cases by simply tolerating higher levels of risk because you have strategies and tactics to manage through those risky circumstances. You will turn more risks into opportunities. Our choice to take calculated risks more often and to turn those risks into opportunities will give us cause for celebration. Women aren't waiting for someone else to grant them permission to take a risk. We have to give ourselves permission. Let's go ahead and do it. Let's increase our propensity for, preparedness for, and likelihood of success with our risk taking. Let's *"Ready, Set...RISK!"* so we can change the choices we make and realize the boundless reservoir of our infinite potential.

Chapter 2: Start Somewhere, Start Now

Fear can paralyze us into inaction. In order to risk, you have to break that cycle. You have to start somewhere, and you have to start now. "Easier said than done," you might think. "Not true," I say. Identify three things you can do to start moving forward, even if they are baby steps. What do you do if you are still well and truly stuck, if you want to take a risk but you are feeling overwhelmed and don't know where to begin and what three things you should do first? Use the following three-step process that has worked for me time and time again to figure it out.

Step One: **Talk about it to others.**

Step Two: **Develop a starter plan that includes the most important milestones you can think of right now.**

Step Three: **Identify a handful of people who can help you move forward with the first few critical aspects of your plan.**

These three steps might sound trite and simple, but do not dismiss them. They are incredibly powerful, irrespective of the magnitude of the risk. It doesn't matter if your end objective morphs, or if your plan evolves, or if the people who you need to surround yourself with change over time. It's not about getting it 100 percent right the first time around. It's about starting somewhere, and starting now!

It is imperative that you embrace a philosophy of "start somewhere, start now" in your risk taking in your career. These three simple steps will help you begin. In the rest of the book we are going to cover strategies and tactics that will aid you in your risk taking, but in order to apply them to you, you have to have something to apply them to.

That's why I am making sure we cover this right out of the gate. You must break beyond the barrier of inaction caused by fear and feeling overwhelmed. You'll figure it out, and it will be OK. You are going to be armed with strategies and tactics to make you better prepared for your risk taking, and that will increase your success with your risk taking. But you have to be willing to start somewhere and start now.

Step One: Talk about it to others.

I had been in the States for eight years by the time I met my husband Steve, and even that is a story about risk taking. I'd had the various boyfriends and fair share of bad relationships that we all have, and had tried a few iterations of the online dating service JDate.com. I had my hard and fast rules when dating, but I took a risk and broke them all with Steve. Two of my biggest rules were "No picture equals no email," and "No meals on a first date"—way too long of a time commitment, and no quick and easy exit strategy if the date was a disaster. Steve had no picture on his profile, but I decided to send him an email anyway, and when he asked me out to dinner for our first date, I accepted. The rest is history—a year and a half later we were married on a beautiful summer day overlooking the Rose Garden at the Chicago Botanic Garden. Steve has been my biggest champion when it comes to the risks I have taken since he has been in my life. When I told him that I wanted to write this book, he said "OK" and he has been there for me every step of the way.

The second person that I told I wanted to write this book was my awesome friend Mike Kaufman. I was standing in the aisle of a Kroger supermarket in Dallas, Texas, and was on the phone with Mike. He and I became friends during the year I spent in Israel. He has known me longer than anyone else in the United States. He also happens to be one of the smartest people I have the privilege of knowing. He recently did his PhD on the subject of success and happiness among executives and other high-achieving professionals, following them from college onward for nearly fifty years. Mike said, "You should do it."

I believed in the concept behind the book, and the person that loved me the most and the person that knew me the longest both believed I could and should do it. I told myself to go ahead, take the risk, and do it. Then I started telling other people whom I trusted and who knew me well that I was going to write this book. The level of interest and support was resoundingly high. It was no longer an "if"—it was a "when" and "how." Telling people made me accountable; it put me on the hook. That's why you have to talk about the risk you are going to take with others. All of sudden people start asking you questions like, "When are you going to start?" or "How are you going to approach it?" The incredible thing is that you will discover you do have answers to many of the questions. Where you don't have answers, talking things through with others will help you to find them. People will get excited, they will help you to move forward, and momentum will pick up on its own accord.

Step Two: Develop a plan that identifies the most important milestones you can think of right now.

You are on your way with the risk you are taking. Now go ahead and develop a high-level plan for yourself that has the most important milestones you can think of at this stage. Brainstorm them out and put them in the order that makes sense at this point in time. Continue to talk with people about your objective and your plan, start working it, and adjust it as you go. The road may be long, you will probably end up adding elements to the plan you did not include initially, and you will most likely change the order of events from what you had originally thought. It does not matter in the least that you have to adjust the plan. The point is that you have a plan you are actually working. Nobody else but you is going to know or care that the road ultimately traveled looks either a little or a lot different than the route you first planned. All that you and anybody else is going to care about is if you moved forward with taking the risk, and if you ultimately arrived at a new destination, whatever that new destination turned out to be. You still moved, and that's a whole lot better than standing still.

I live this iterative plan-execute-amend cycle every time I take a risk. It always plays out a little differently. Having a plan to work

against always infuses confidence in yourself and others around your
risk taking. When I recognized I might want to leave Deloitte and not
stay to become a Partner in the firm, my plan had the following high-
level milestones: Hire an executive coach to aid me in thinking through
this objectively, make my dilemma known to key people who know
me well and that I trust inside and outside Deloitte so that I can have
open and honest conversations with them as I think through this, keep
on track with current project assignments as I will need those sales
numbers and work-managed numbers should I decide to stay, and
actively explore what options could look like for me in a life outside of
Deloitte. Although some people may not have been happy with my
ultimate decision, no one could fault me for the diligence I applied as
I executed on my plan. My plan also engendered confidence in myself
and others that, despite the risk I was taking, I knew exactly what I
was doing.

**Step Three: Identify a handful of people who can help you
move forward with the first few critical aspects of
your plan.**

There are people in your circle who can help you move forward with
your risk taking. You just need to ask them for their help. There will
be some surprises—some good, some not. There will be people who
you could have sworn would do anything they possibly could to help
you who will disappoint you because they won't lift a finger. There
will be people who you could never have imagined in your wildest
dreams would go as far above and beyond for you as they do. That's
OK; everyone has his or her reasons. But the fact is that you don't need
every single person to step up. You just need a critical mass. You will
find that critical mass. Just keep asking until you do.

When I decided I wanted to launch a program to companies in the
Chicago marketplace focused on cross-generational collaboration as a
strategy for development and advancement of women in the workplace,
I told people about it, I developed my plan, and then I mined my
network to help me get out the starting gate. I leveraged my network
to learn about and find the right vendors to hire to build out the

infrastructure I needed. I told everyone I knew and everyone I met about what I was doing, and I asked them to help me with getting introductions to the people in their companies that make decisions about investing in developing their female talent. If they were the decision-makers, I asked them to consider sending women on the program. I asked people to support me in ways that didn't necessarily require them to expend hard dollars but that were key to the success of the program, such as being a guest speaker. I asked, and although many people said no, a critical mass said yes. The program was a great success in its pilot year, and I am now headed into the second year of the program with a new class that has grown both in terms of core participants and the companies sending those participants.

A critical mass of people helped me to gain momentum with some of the first key aspects of my plan. They helped me to get started, and steam picked up from there. Whatever risk you are going to embark upon, you have those people too. Just ask them for what you need from them. You do not need to go it alone. *"Ready, Set...RISK!"* is in your hands right now as a result of me starting somewhere, starting now with this three-step process. Writing this book was indeed a risk for me on many fronts, and it would have been easy to get stuck by feeling overwhelmed at the enormity of what I was undertaking. "Start somewhere, start now" helped me to turn my risk into opportunity and reality. Adopting a philosophy of "start somewhere, start now" enabled me to talk about my concept and vision with others, develop a plan early on with the most critical milestones, and identify the people who could help me move forward with the plan.

The most critical group of people who helped me move forward is those individuals who agreed to be interviewed for the book. It is the stories, insights, and perspectives they shared with me during the interview process that bring this book alive. These amazing, wonderful, and generous people shared their time and their stories, and were critical in steps one and three above, in whichever iteration of the process I was in. These are all people who have taken significant risks in their careers. These are all people who started somewhere, started now, have exciting results to show for it, and who have superb insights to share on the subject of women and risk taking. Without further ado, let me introduce you to the incredible cast of characters that you'll be hearing from throughout the book.

Kim Waller, Executive Vice President at Willis North America, and Diane Gillespie, Vice President, Digital Marketing at OnCourse Learning, are two amazing ladies who got involved at the very beginning, when I was writing my sample chapters. Kim and I first got to know each other when we were both at another major insurance brokerage firm. Kim is a trailblazer, changing the model for how companies work with minority- and women-owned businesses. Diane and I got to know each other in my spinning classes. I am a certified group exercise instructor, and I teach a killer group cycle class. Diane risks every Saturday when she comes to my ninety-minute endurance class. Diane's career risk taking started when she was a teenager and became one of the first girl caddies to work the golf courses in the Midwest.

There are other friends and budding friends that said "of course" without even blinking an eyelid when I asked to interview them. Janet (Jan) Allen is President/CEO of PayTech, whom I met when I was doing a software vendor evaluation and selection for a law firm client. Jan founded PayTech fifteen years ago, and it is now a strategic partner with many of the large Human Capital Management software vendors. Erin Duffy is Area Vice President—Public Sector Practice, Health and Welfare Consulting at Arthur J. Gallagher & Co. (Gallagher), who in turn also secured the involvement of Leslie Lemenager, Vice President responsible for international business and global growth of the Benefits and HR Consulting division of Gallagher. I met Erin at one of the G-WATT dinners I organize every few months. Erin is a fast-rising star at Gallagher, an impressive young woman in her late twenties, advised and mentored by Leslie. Leslie is a senior leader who views it as part of her responsibility to help Erin and others like Erin be as successful as they can be, and to make her eligible for as many candidate pools as possible by helping to prepare her to take calculated risks. Just a couple of years younger than Erin, Katie Zupancic is a Marketing Coordinator at Event 360. I started advising Katie when she moved to Chicago after graduating from Vanderbilt University; to me she epitomizes the risk taker who finds a way to stand out from the crowd. When Katie was interviewing for jobs in Chicago, she followed up her phone interviews at Event 360 by hand-delivering size-ten shoes to the interviewers with a note saying that she was excited to take the next step with them in her career. Then there is Sue Duckett. Like me, Sue carries her accent with her wherever she goes, except that hers is a British accent. Sue, Managing Director of Bibby Financial Services—a global factoring and finance solutions company—moved from the United Kingdom to the United States in 2011 to head up and grow the US factoring business.

There are women you will hear from whom I have met fairly recently, who were thrilled when I told them about the book and immediately answered "yes" when I asked them if they would be interested in being interviewed. Connie Lindsey is Executive Vice President, and Head of Corporate Social Responsibility and Global Diversity and Inclusion at Northern Trust. Connie is also Immediate Past National Board President of Girl Scouts of the USA, the highest-ranking volunteer of this 3.4 million–member organization. Annette Reid—another Brit who moved to the United States a few years ago—is now Head of Talent Management at a US-based Insurance company with approximately 7,500 employees, prior to which she was Senior Vice President of Global Organization Development at Aviva. We met over dinner one night prior to a Carrie Underwood concert we were attending at the same venue and immediately hit it off. Melanie Sabelhaus is the Founder and CEO of Exclusive Interim Properties (EIP). EIP merged with four other companies to form BridgeStreet Worldwide—making Melanie one of the cofounders—and the company did an IPO and went public on the NASDAQ in 1997. At one stage Melanie was Deputy Administrator of the US Small Business Administration. She is also the founding national cochair of Tiffany Circle at the Red Cross, and she is currently Vice Chair of the National American Red Cross. Melanie and I met through my agent. Margaret (Peg) Anderson and I met when I was the featured speaker at a Turnaround Management Association event in Chicago. Peg is a Capital Partner in the law firm of Fox, Swibel, Levin & Carroll, LLP. I met Nancy Sharp when I was a keynote speaker at a day conference organized by the Society of Human Resource Management in Chicago.

Nancy is President of Food For Thought—a leading provider of fine catering, cafeterias, and conference catering. She cofounded the company in 1983. Maureen Larson is Partner, Lettuce Parties & Special Events and The Ivy Room, Lettuce Entertain You Restaurants—a group of eighty-three restaurants. Maureen and I met when I approached Lettuce to look at venues of theirs for the cross-generation collaboration program I run for companies in Chicago. Meetings with Maureen are especially fun—she always makes sure you are well fed.

My network was a vital source of additional introductions—in some cases to people whom I wanted to interview but didn't know, so I asked my contacts if they would be willing to make introductions. In other cases people in my network offered up names and introductions to individuals whom they were adamant would want to be interviewed, so more folks came to the table. Janet Lee, who is Vice President of Legal at HERE, a Nokia company. Melinda Hall—Founder and President, TransitionPoint Human Resources. In the reverse of what Sue and Annette and myself did—moving from other countries to the United States—Janet spent a couple of years living and working in Russia, and Melinda spent a number of years living and working in the United Kingdom. Nancy Mueller is Executive Vice President– Chief Operations Officer at Zurich North America. Nancy in turn facilitated introductions to two other amazing women at Zurich North America for me to interview—Karen McDonald and Jennifer Kyung. Karen is Head of Talent Management, and Jennifer is Senior Vice President, Operations. Jennifer is also Zurich North America's Headquarters Business Lead, and she heads up their Women's Initiative. Toni Marnul is a Creative Director at a global consumer product goods company. I told Toni when I met with her how fun it is for me to get to know people who work with tangible products that we all know and touch, since everything I do is so much more abstract in nature. Jon Anderson, Managing Director at China Focus, was the first gentleman I interviewed. Jon subsequently introduced me to my first interviewee who is not a US citizen, and who lives and works outside of the United States—Jane Feng (Feng Yanyan), who goes by the name of Yanyan. Yanyan is an entrepreneur, founder of SN Mandarin-Your Reliable Language Partner—a Chinese language training school for foreigners in China. Last but not least, Pamela (Pam) Durkin and Francene Pelmon. Pam recently retired from ADP, where she was Vice President West National Accounts. Francene is a Senior Consultant at University of Illinois Business Innovation Services.

Companies as a whole stepped forward as well. It's one thing when you want to interview someone specific at a company. It's another thing when you want to interview someone at a company, but you don't have a specific name in mind. Points of contact at AT&T, Aon, BDO USA, BP, and Citi Retail Services all stepped up to help me navigate their organizations and land with the right people to be interviewed.

Debbie Storey, Senior Vice President, Talent Development and Chief Diversity Officer at AT&T, agreed to be interviewed. Featured in Sylvia Ann Hewlett's recent book *Forget a Mentor, Find a Sponsor: The New Way to Fast-Track Your Career* (Harvard Business Review Press, 2013), Debbie was thrilled about the concept of a book on women and risk taking in their professional careers. At Aon, a prior colleague whom I had fairly recently reconnected with after we both joined the Board of Directors at the Chicago Sinfonietta reached across the oceans to Bindu Krishnan. Bindu is ex-Service Delivery Leader, HRBPO Asia-Pacific, Aon Hewitt. BP secured me wonderful interviewees in three countries. You'll hear from Roger Edwards, Country Sales Manager, United Kingdom and Ireland, BP Lubricants; Mukta Tandon, Senior Brand Communications Manager, BP, PLC; and Vladlena (Vlada) Boukhareva—Retail Sales Manager, Russia, at Castrol Russia. At BDO USA, LLP, two people willingly stepped forward. The first was Wayne Berson, CEO and Chairman of the Global Board. A fellow South African, the interview started with that easy flow of sharing where we grew up, looking for any common South African connections (we didn't have any), and concluded with me promising to send Wayne some of my homemade biltong (our South African version of beef jerky). Catherine (Cathy) Moy is BDO's Chief People Officer, and Office Managing Partner Boston, Assurance Services. One of the women participating in my cross-generational collaboration program in Chicago—gen-xyb™ High Tea—from Citi

Retail Services secured the participation of Antonio (Tony) Castañon, Managing Director, Citi Retail Services. Tony leads Citi Retail Services's largest client relationship—Sears.

Every single one of these amazing people brings with them a passion for the topic and a purpose for what they want to share with you, the reader. Their stories are unvarnished, straight from the heart and the head, and fascinating. Different ages, different genders, different places in their career paths, different countries, they all embody the spirit and voice the cheer *"Ready, Set...RISK!"* So grab something to drink and a snack, settle in for a good read, and enjoy visiting with them as you turn the pages ahead.

Chapter 3: Stretching Yourself on Your Risk-taking Continuums

John F. Ross discusses the myth of zero risk in his book *The Polar Bear Strategy—Reflections on Risk in Modern Life*. He explains the myth of zero risk as follows: "Whenever an action is taken to reduce a risk in one area, a risk or risks in another area will be heightened...A risk cannot be assessed and managed along only one dimension...In fact, risk management, both individually and collectively, involves a world of trade-offs and demands a certain finesse."[1]

The myth of zero risk applies to us as women in our careers. When faced with a choice to do something new, something that has risk associated with it, it is imperative that you contemplate that career risk thoughtfully and thoroughly. If you choose what appears to be the safe alternative—which you may tell yourself is the path of zero risk because you are concerned about the risk associated with the other option—then you are deluding yourself. You must accept that there are risks associated with all the options. When you start thinking about the experiences you risk not being part of, what you won't end up learning, who you won't end up getting exposure to, what you risk losing in earning potential, when you think about all the opportunities you risk losing out on by following the safe path and not taking calculated risk—then you understand the relevance of the myth of zero risk. Indeed one of the most basic but also incredibly valuable exercises you can do for yourself when evaluating your options is to do a side-by-side comparison of the risks and opportunities, the pros and the cons associated with each of the various options you are considering.

You can even take this one step further. We all hate to lose, right? To truly evaluate if the risk at hand is a good idea or not, you need to understand how the fact that you hate to lose colors your lenses when you consider taking a risk, how it influences the pros and cons you might list in the exercise above, and how you might react to them when reading them back to yourself. Doug Sundheim talks about this in his book *Taking Smart Risks*. He highlights the need to choose the right focus for risk taking, bringing up research conducted in the 1970s by two cognitive psychologists, Daniel Kahneman and Amos Tversky. He shares how they identified what they called loss-aversion bias—that human beings hate to lose, and that we will do almost anything we can to avoid losing, even if the actions we take as a result are not in our best interests. The implication is explained by Sundheim as follows: "When you choose to focus on what you might lose by taking risks—that is, what you already have...—it makes risk taking seem like a bad idea. When you choose to focus on what you might lose by *not* taking risks—that is, what you *don't* already have...—it makes risk taking look like a smart idea."[2] I encourage you to repeat the side-by-side comparison exercise with this different set of lenses on. You will be pleasantly surprised at the additional insights you glean for yourself.

You can't stop there. You need to push yourself even further on this. While we can certainly appreciate that risk management demands the skill and ability to constantly evaluate and conduct a balancing act, it looks and feels different depending on where each of us stands on our own personal risk-taking continuums. Risk-taking continuums are a very important part of the language of risk. You need to understand where you stand on risk-taking continuums, and why. Where you are this month or this year with regards to your appetite and preparedness for risk in your career may be quite different from where you are next month or next year. You must acknowledge where you currently stand on those risk-taking continuums versus where you want to be. You must also recognize which risk-taking continuums apply. Circumstances change. You change.

You can turn risk into opportunity by managing your movement along the continuums using the strategies and tactics we cover in Part II of *"Ready, Set...RISK!"* Speaking the language of risk empowers you to shift your position on the continuums, to shape your own destiny by stretching yourself further than you have gone before on those continuums. There is neither a right nor a wrong in terms of placement on these continuums. What matters is an honest self-assessment of where you are versus where you need to be. The continuums in this chapter are not the only ones that are relevant in the context of risk taking in your career. You should self-identify others that are pertinent to your situation.

Risk analysis science has shown us that we all have our own "mental models"—a whole host of hidden, informal rules and assumptions that we each subconsciously apply to risk-related decisions. Exploring continuums will help you to challenge your thinking, raise questions, and find answers that will enable you to change assumptions and rules you are applying to your risk-related decisions. Also, keep in mind the principal of expected utility maximization, which quite simply is that an individual will incur risks in proportion to the benefits the person expects to reap as a result of taking those risks, and recognize that typically you can tolerate higher levels of risk from something that you choose for yourself. So as you move yourself along the continuums, think of the benefits you will derive and remember this is all of your own choosing. Don't let misleading notions about risk maneuver you into not taking risks. Instead make your choice about where you want to be and then develop strategies to navigate through risk.

We will examine six stretch continuums in this chapter:

1   Blend in with the crowd...Stand out from the crowd

2   Move away from something...Move towards something

3   Do well...Realize my full potential

4   Focus on my skill gaps...Play to my strengths

5   Maintain steady state...Change

6   Be what others need me to be...Stay true to myself

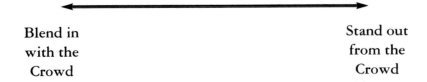

Blend in
with the
Crowd

Stand out
from the
Crowd

Do you feel more comfortable adhering to the general norms, blending in with the crowd, and generally not rocking the boat? How comfortable are you with putting yourself out there, standing apart from the crowd, and voicing your opinion, even if it is contrary to consensus held by others? There are times when it is good to go with the flow. But when you want to take a risk, you need to be willing, and you need to prepare yourself to stand out from the crowd. Risk takers are going to be in the spotlight sooner rather than later and more often than not. So when it's time for you to risk, you will need to adjust your positioning on the continuum, even if just for a short while.

Diane had no qualms about taking a risk in pursuing an opportunity where she would clearly stand out from the crowd. Diane is the eldest of four children. Her father was a painter/wall-paperer and one of nine siblings, none of who went to college. College for his kids was very important to him, even if it was a struggle financially. She shared her story with me over lunch one day. "One day he was painting a country club and he came home with an application for my brother to be a caddy, and me and my sister said, 'Oh, can we do that too?' He said, 'I don't think they allow girls to caddy, but we can go to the country club and ask.' So we went to the country club that was fifteen or twenty minutes away from our house and my father went and asked. Then he brought us in, and we went in front of some type of a board or association for the country club, and they said, 'Yes, girls can come.' I would have been thirteen or so around 1979. There was another caddy there—the top caddy—and he had a sister. Once he found out they were going to allow girls she came as well. So it was me and my one sister and this other girl."

Diane ended up getting an Evans Scholarship from the Evans Scholars Foundation. The Western Golf Association's championships rank among the oldest and most prestigious in the United States. They use their tournament legacy and reputation to further their charitable mission: the Evans Scholars Foundation, which awards college scholarships to caddies from modest means. Diane and her sister could have taken another path, a path where they blended in with the crowd—that might have been perceived to be of zero risk. But instead, when faced with a choice to do something new, something that had risk associated with it because it required them to put themselves out there and pursue something that was not a norm for girls at that time, they did it.

←————————————————————————————→

**Move away   Move towards
from something   something**

If something isn't working out right and you want to move away from it, that could trigger you to consider taking a risk and making a change. However, moving away from something and letting go of what is known to you can be hard. Like Sundheim explained—you know what you have to lose. The key on this continuum is to define what it is that you are reaching out for and grabbing on to. Part of that is establishing the "why" in your risk taking—what are the underlying factors driving you to change things up? The other part is putting specifics to "what" it is you are aiming to accomplish, the benefits associated with the risk, and recognizing what you currently don't have and likely never will have if you don't take a risk. Establishing what you are moving towards will also reduce concerns that if you take the risk you could end up in a situation that is worse than what you are in right now. Like the gymnast on the uneven bars that lets go of one bar and reaches out to grab the other bar, or the rock climber that releases a fingertip-grip on one rock hold to stretch up and hook into the next hold on the route, risking letting go doesn't seem so scary if you know what you are moving towards. In Mukta's eyes, "The risk becomes doubled if I am running away from something because I might end up [with] something that will be worse than what I already had. But if I am moving towards something I really want, then the risk is half what everybody else perceives as the risk. So for me, my life has been am I running away from something or am I running towards something? If I am running towards something it will all turn out fine. It's not really going to be a risk in the long run."

Perceptions around your position on this continuum also count. In general people will buy into and support you in your risk taking more so if they know you are driven by both what you are moving away and what you are moving towards. Annette told a story about a juncture she reached in her career with Aviva—a global life and general insurance company headquartered in the United Kingdom. After ten years in Operations she was starting to think about where to go from here. She had increased her leadership responsibilities significantly and was given another promotion, but at the same time an opportunity came up to move into Human Resources. Given that the things she loved the most were about growing and developing people, seeing them thrive, understanding different aspects of leadership, and bringing the best out of people, she felt it would be great to move into an HR role, particularly with the background of ten years in the business.

Annette shared how other people in the company questioned her taking this risk. "The risk was the role wasn't graded the same as the role I had just gotten. The bands were so broad it wasn't going to impact my salary, but it was the perception of taking a lower role. My gut instinct was, 'This will get corrected quite quickly. I'll get myself in the area I want to be in. I'll be able to prove myself. I'll be able to jump back up again fairly quickly.' But there were a lot of people with raised eyebrows thinking, 'Why on earth would she do this? Why would she take a step down to go into HR when things are looking great for her career within the branch?' But I stuck with it because I just had this feeling that was where my passion and energy would be going forward, and that I could really add a lot of value with the knowledge I had gained over the ten years. There were so many raised eyebrows that even the Chief Human Resources Officer decided to interview me to ask, 'What is your motivation; are you running away from something?' Which of course I wasn't. I had just decided I wanted to do something else. I have never looked back. HR has absolutely become my working home. My opportunities in HR have been huge."

Do well   **Realize my**
                                                              full potential

Doing well is great. What doing well means can be defined in so many different ways for each person, and it can change over time. You might be at a point in your life and career where doing well based on your definition of doing well is extremely satisfying to you and enough for now. But for many of you doing well is not enough, and you want to realize your full potential. In most cases that requires you to take a risk, maybe even multiple risks. I had meetings recently with two women who are in this exact situation. For the one lady, shifting where she resides on this risk-taking continuum is going to require her investing time over the next six to twelve months actively discovering the world of opportunities available to her inside and outside her current organization, and defining more clearly what it is she wants to move towards, even as she continues to perform well in her current role. For the other lady, shifting her position on this continuum is going to require her to change how she positions herself in the marketplace as she searches for a new job opportunity, and to get more comfortable talking about herself and claiming the "I" in her accomplishments to date. The rewards associated with realizing your full potential are so gratifying, but you can only reap them if you take a risk to discover what you are really capable of and then take the necessary risks to get there. In taking those risks, your journey towards realizing your full potential may even mean that for a short while you aren't doing as well as you were before (again based on your own definition of what doing well means to you), because you are stretching yourself and you are learning how to do this new thing you have taken a risk on.

Peg and I share a common thread in our career paths. Both of us voluntarily left the large companies at which we were doing well to forge risky but ultimately exciting and successful new paths elsewhere. In Peg's case she was leaving a very large law firm where she was a Partner. In my case I was leaving Deloitte Consulting in the year that, for all intents and purposes, looked like it would be my final step in the journey towards Partner. Peg and I traded stories. We shared how we had grappled with staying where we were clearly doing well and could continue to do well, but how at the same time we felt that while we were certainly appreciated, we were not fully valued for everything that we could possibly be and therefore would never realize our full potential if we stayed. Our stretch on this continuum became not settling for just doing well but rather taking the big, brave, bold steps towards realizing our full potential, even if that was scary, traumatic, and certainly risky. We have both found huge bounce in our moves. Peg said to me during the course of the interview, "For me taking the risk of changing law firms has worked out economically. It has worked out as far as quality of work I am doing. But where it's really worked out has been allowing me to be fully me, and that has been just a wonderful gift."

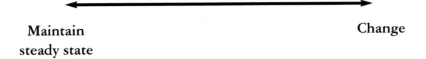

Maintain   **Change**
steady state

There is a time in everyone's life and career when maintaining steady state is the right thing. It's certainly also a very comfortable thing to do. Taking risk requires willingness to change and the ability to handle those changes. If you want to take a risk, and you believe it is the right time for you to risk, best you get ready to deal with a lot of change and put the infrastructure and support in place around you to help you through the change. Just like realizing your full potential, being adept at handling change is incredibly rewarding, and the more you can do it the more successful you will be in your risk taking.

Perspectives on this came up with almost everyone I interviewed. Connie said, "I think along three tracks…The third [track] is the risk of staying the same, the risk of not growing, the risk of not changing. There is a quote by Will Rogers: 'Even if you're on the right track you'll get run over if you just sit there.' So the risk of staying the same is to me the biggest risk." Cathy described it as, "You're going to reach those points where you say this has been great for the last ten years, but do the next ten look like the last ten? Do the next five look like the last five? That's a draining thought. I don't find that comforting for me." Maureen tells her daughter, "If you don't take that risk, you'll never know. But if you don't you are quite probably going to be stuck in that same place. It is only going to get worse for you because now you know. You have this seed in your head and the longer you don't deal with it the worse it's going to get for you. The old saying—If you always do what you've always done you'll always get what you've always gotten. That rings in my head all the time." Nancy Mueller spoke about not having regrets. Fairly early in her career, a Senior Vice President at the company she was at took a new opportunity at AIG and asked her to follow. But the opportunity was in New Hampshire. Nancy shared what her thoughts were at the time. "Should I stay? I'm not unhappy. Or should I take this chance, and move us to New Hampshire? Move a spouse that's working, and what does that do? We wanted to have children, so there's that whole piece. I decided to go. What's the worst that can happen? That's the whole risk thing. It felt safer to stay. But then as we talked though it, it really was five years from now, ten years from now, will I regret it? The 'I wish we would have done something,' or 'I wish I would have,' was to me not something I wanted to experience."

Yanyan spoke of her friends, family, teachers, and students in China as falling into one of three groups. One group is happy with their current life. One group doesn't know what they want and don't give it much thought. The third group is not satisfied with their current life. She said, "They are not happy. They don't enjoy life. They feel life has no hope. They kind of know what they should do, and kind of know what they really hope [for], but they fear the risk thing. They

know to do one kind of thing to make themselves happy, but they dare
not to try. Although the current situation is not that good, the change
makes them even more anxious. They need courage [to change]."

<!-- arrow -->

Focus on my   **Play to my**
  skill gaps   **strengths**

When it's time to risk in your career, conduct a very honest self-
assessment to see how far to the right you are on this continuum. You
have a much greater chance of success if the particular risk you are
considering taking plays to your leading strengths and your natural
talents. If indeed it does, those strengths will help you accelerate to
the endgame faster and recover from bumps in the road quicker. Across
the board you will feel less exposed. That doesn't mean you should
ignore areas where you may have skill gaps, but rather that you should
be creative to find ways to mitigate the exposure you might have
during the course of your risk taking because of them. Furthermore
your strengths should be such an integral part of your personal brand
that it is very apparent to others which risks you are well suited for,
making you a leading contender for those types of opportunities,
because people know you have a high likelihood of success with that
risk.

Early in Debbie's career—when she was in her mid-twenties—the
President of the company she was at asked her to move out of the
customer service organization and take over the sales organization. She
had no background in sales. She had never been in sales in that business
or any other business. The sales organization was comprised of a group
of men who had been selling printing for anywhere between twenty-
eight and thirty-five years. It was a very intimidating prospect.

Her first reaction was, "Why me? I don't know how to do this." She
spoke to her mentor. "What do I do about this? I've been asked to step
in and go and take over sales, and I'm not qualified for that. I'm not
equipped for that...I haven't done it before, and I have no experience."

Her mentor's response was, "You need to think about why he's asking you to take over sales. It's obviously not because you're an expert in sales. It's because of the skills you've demonstrated in the jobs that you've had leading up to this." Debbie decided to take the risk and pursue the opportunity because she realized she'd be leading with her strengths, and her strengths had become a huge part of her personal brand. She commented, "I am very passionate about the establishment of a personal brand. Even at that time in my career I had established a brand that really carried with me throughout my career. That's what I've always re-grounded on. I've always said to myself, 'I'm not being put in this position because I know network architecture, or because I know how to run an IT organization. I'm being put in this position because of my reputation, which reflects my strengths and brand.' I always had a conversation with myself before stepping into a new role. 'Remember what your strengths are. Remember why they're important in this role and know how you'll use them.'"

Be what others   **Stay true to**
need me to be   **myself**

It's hard to risk when you are investing energy into trying to be what others want you to be, if that is not your authentic self. Risk requires you to stretch yourself out of your comfort zone, and it's easier to do that when you are operating from your core and staying true to yourself. If the risk you are considering taking in your career is anchored around compromising yourself and/or others, that doesn't bode well. The chances of success when taking calculated risks in your career is vastly increased if you are coming from a place where you can be your authentic yourself and where your actions and words honestly represent the essence of who you are.

Connie shared "I am a very goals-driven person. I understand that there are things we have to be willing to risk. I never risk values. I never risk my core belief that all human beings are created equal. ... There are boundaries; there are lines beyond which I will not go. I will not take a risk that is going to either inadvertently or otherwise do irreparable harm to someone. I am not going to make a business decision that is going to harm the organization or the broader goals for which I'm working...I am not willing to risk integrity for performance or anything that will have a longer term deleterious impact on the organization, my team or my personal reputation." Janet spoke about the importance of staying true to your course and to yourself in order to be successful in your risk taking. "People and points of view come in and out of favor...People can get very confused or try to sway with the wind a lot. If you are true to your course, then that is your deepest asset. That's how you weather the low spots. You see people like Steve Jobs as an extreme example. Ultimately he had it so deep in him to stay the course he started at the beginning."

Willingness to risk and having success in your risk taking in your career also requires you to be proud of who you are and what you stand for, and to be willing to take a firm stand against any compromises in order to stay true to yourself. Sometimes it even requires you to make a leap, and it's a lot easier to take a risky leap if you are staying true to who you are. On a sunny afternoon, sipping tea and looking south over Chicago from a meeting room at the Metropolitan Club in Willis Tower, Kim shared a story of hers, which epitomizes this. "In one case I was the Managing Director for an operating unit. I had been promoted into that position at a time that entity had already hit financially challenging times, where its business model was subject to being questioned [as to] whether or not it worked in that corporate construct. There were a couple of things that went on when I was named Managing Director. I was told by someone, 'Teams aren't going to want to report to you because you are a black female.' " I looked up at Kim in surprise when she shared this with me. She nodded her head, widened her eyes, smiled wryly, and shared with me her response to that individual. She said to him, "The senior executive team has decided they want me to run this division. I am a black female and that's not going to change, so we will all have to find a way to work together. That is always going to be the case."

Kim felt the remark was intended to get her off her game, and that she had to choose between two different scenarios, both risky. One scenario was to fold and say, "You know what—you are right. I think I can't do this." There was no way she was going to do that. The second scenario was to rise to the challenge, dig her heels in, and take the role regardless of the potential opposition, because she knew the attitude was wrong. She said to the gentleman concerned, "OK, here's the deal. If there is someone that decides they no longer want to work here because they can't find a way to work for me that is absolutely their choice." Kim stayed true to herself and everything that she valued within herself, stepping into the position with her head held high, not apologetic in the least for who she was.

The uphill battle continued over the next six years. The business model continued to face challenges, leading Kim to suggest multiple times to the senior leadership team that they sell the business and take care of the employees in a managed transition. But she was literally told that they would not sell it off—even if they had to release everyone but her and two other people to run the operating unit. It finally got to the point where Kim had to make a difficult decision. She had to make the right—albeit difficult—decision from a business perspective. She decided to resign from her position. In doing so it would make a re-organization almost inevitable which would most likely lead to a re-evaluation of the sale of the unit and transition arrangements for the remaining employees. Kim concluded her story. "I knew that was a risk, but I knew I could no longer pretend. For me the risk was tempered because I felt like there was no other option for me to take...That scary jump becomes less scary when you factor in what really are your viable alternatives for you to take. If there aren't any then you have to take that jump. If you are in a burning building and on the ledge, and there is no way out, you can sit there and burn up, or you can have enough courage and leap."

Chapter 3 Notes

1   Ross, John F. *The Polar Bear Strategy—Reflections on Risk in Modern Life.* Perseus Books, 1999: 148.

2   Sundheim, Doug. *Taking Smart Risks.* McGraw Hill, 2013: 19–21.

Chapter 4: An Important Conversation

Who tends to get the top jobs in a company? Risk takers do. I'm not talking about wild, careless, over-the-edge-of-the-cliff kind of risk takers who are willing to bet their entire career, the fortune of the whole company, and the livelihood of all employees, on perilous decisions. I'm talking about the kind of person that you and I all know—the kind of person who inspires us when we hear them tell their story, and who we admire for their insight, courage, fortitude, and skills.

We admire their ability to assess a situation, read the inputs, identify the opportunity and associated risks, make tough decisions, and then take consecutive, smart, calculated risks, with success being the outcome more often than not. We admire them for their ability to engage others in the planning and execution around risks, and for their skill in bringing others along with them on the journey. We respect them for owning their decisions, irrespective of the outcome, and their ability to pick themselves up, dust themselves off, and do it differently if it doesn't work out quite right the first time. For the most part we really like these people, especially the risk takers who get the top jobs and continue to retain and display the same characteristics that made them relatable and inspiring to others in the first place—motivated go-getters with lofty goals, exciting ideas, expertise, and confidence in their ability to secure successful outcomes, and with a fair share of competency gaps, realistic concerns, and a healthy dash of humility. People like that rise to the top of an organization. Real people like that are the risk takers.

In an article in a 1978 edition of *Management Review* titled "Risk-taking managers: Who gets the top jobs?" Dr. Ronald J. Grey and Dr. George G. Gordon shared some of their findings on this subject. "Those who rise to the top of an organization *do* tend to be the risk takers...One reason for the rapid upward mobility of risk-oriented individuals may be their ability to produce highly successful business results...Success in this instance was reflected in both the bottom line and effectiveness in managing people." [1] They found that risk-taking motivation appears to be an early indicator of future success, and people who score higher on risk-taking propensity tend to be identified as top candidates for advancement more often than those who score lower on risk taking. They pointed out that risk takers tend to hire their own kind. They identified some of the characteristics exhibited by risk takers: seeing limits of authority as less well defined, wanting to more frequently make decisions on their own, and having a good deal of personal accountability.[1]

That's you! You just need to recognize it in yourself and step into these shoes. Furthermore, the people described above are also working with you and for you in your organization. Leaders in companies need to recognize this so that they can channel calculated risk taking to maximum positive effect. From both a personal and an organizational perspective, conversations on women and risk taking are exciting and important conversations to have, because individuals and the organization will both benefit. So how do you have those conversations? You can start with the following four themes:

Recognize and address perceptions around women and risk taking in their career.

Acknowledge and leverage the benefits of the female factor at work in the marketplace.

Recognize and address cultural factors that may influence the career risks women take.

Appreciate and account for how risk taking in one's career fits in the broader landscape of life.

Recognize and address <u>perceptions</u> around women and risk taking in their career.

Perception is reality. You have your perception of your own appetite and tolerance for taking risks in your career. In turn, others have their perceptions of your risk-taking propensity and resilience. Perceptions influence the opportunities you see for yourself and the opportunities that others see for you—the risks you take and the risks that others take on you, with you and for you. It is important to consider this as you plan and execute your calculated risk taking. Recognize the perceptions that exist, and where necessary take action to change those perceptions.

In one of Annette's HR roles at Aviva she started working with global teams. That led to the opportunity to move to the United States. But that opportunity almost didn't come about—because of perceptions. It all unfolded during a conversation with her manager about what was next. Annette told him she was starting to think about an international move, which almost stopped him in his tracks. He said to her, "You know, Annette, the perception in the organization about you is you're not mobile." Annette recognized that people were talking about her at talent reviews in the context of opportunities in other countries, but were under the impression she was not mobile. Nobody had spoken to her about it. Earlier in her career she wasn't mobile, but that had changed a while back. About three weeks after actively correcting the perception, she got a call saying, "We're setting up our Aviva regional office in Chicago. We want somebody to come over and lead Talent Management and Organizational Development." They wanted Annette.

Misperceptions around satisfaction levels and risk tolerance can fool an organization into being complacent regarding key talent, often resulting in negative consequences. After being at Lettuce Entertain You for twenty-two years, Maureen got frustrated when greater business opportunities didn't come to fruition, despite many conversations with key stakeholders over the better part of a year and a half. Lettuce is heavily spearheaded by male leadership. So when another company reached out to Maureen with an opportunity to come on board and help them take their company to the next level, and offered to bring her in as an equity partner, she took them up on it. "I left Lettuce after twenty-two years. That was a huge risk for me. Major. I think about it sometimes, and I think, 'Holy cow! I can't believe I did it!'...I am divorced. I am the primary breadwinner. I honestly don't think they thought I was going to leave. I think they were surprised."

I smiled ruefully as Maureen told her story, because I experienced the same thing when I left Deloitte. I loved being at Deloitte, I was focused on making Partner, and I was successful there. Going back to the risk continuums we discussed in the prior chapter, their perception of me was that I wanted to continue to be one of the Deloitte crowd, not that I wanted to stand apart. Their perception was that doing well was what it was all about for me; they did not recognize how important realizing my full potential was to me. They were more focused on the importance of me closing any skill gaps they perceived necessary to finish up the Partner process and sticking with the core competencies for which I was known—i.e., maintain steady state. I was more focused on playing to my strengths and reinventing myself with new things— i.e., changing and growing. Their perception was that there was no way I would risk leaving at this point in the game. They were wrong. My perception was that there was no way I could risk staying. My perceptions and Deloitte's of where I was on those risk-taking continuums was vastly different. There was a lot of open dialog between us as I evaluated whether to leave or not—but even though they tried very hard to get me to stay, it was too little, too late, as I realized I was at the point of no return. I left. Perhaps if those key differences in perception had been recognized and worked on years earlier by both parties, there would have been a different outcome.

There is an interesting twist and outcome in Maureen's story. Not too long after her departure, Lettuce Entertain You reached out to Maureen and asked her to come back, which she indeed did decide to do. She told me the ending of the story. "They had found an opportunity where they wanted me to head up the project as a Partner...I think they had realized what was missing after I left. What I am working through [now] is going at things with a different way of respect, actually, because I took the risk."

Perceptions influence who's on the list of candidates for those risky-but-top opportunities. In addition to the South African connection that Wayne and I share, we also share the experience and insight that comes with building your career in a large professional services firm. Using fictitious names, Wayne commented on the importance of senior leaders in an organization actively and publicly managing perceptions. "Part of what happens is that people will say, 'Oh, Daniella doesn't do this because she goes home early, and Tom is here till late at night while Daniella is home watching TV. That's not fair.' So the way we counter that is that we say, 'Well, Daniella's jobs got no comments, and Tom's job got five comments. Daniella's jobs are profitability level of X. Tom's jobs are X minus something.' So we point out that it's not always what you see on the outside. Highlight success stories as well." By recognizing people in front of their peers and actively managing perceptions, BDO is laying the groundwork for everyone—male and female—to have a fair shot at being considered for the high-risk, high-reward opportunities.

In Chapter 1 I shared that in general people's perception is that women take career-related risks less frequently than men. Publicly acknowledging your risk taking helps to overcome this generalization. Peg said, "Society's view is that women are averse to taking risk, and I don't think that's true at all. I think the form of risk, or how we approach risk as a whole, is probably different for women than for men. Our risk taking is probably not quite as dramatic, but it doesn't mean it's not risk taking. It's partly because women do a very bad job of blowing their own horn. When men take risk, they are much more vocal about the fact they are taking risk. This is a stereotype, but women are also a little less impulsive than men, and the risks that women take tend to be a little bit more thought out, and therefore maybe aren't perceived as being risky, because you've weighed the alternatives. [However] the fact that you weighed the alternatives beforehand and thought about it doesn't mean it's not a risk."

Acknowledge and leverage the benefits of the <u>female factor</u> at work in the marketplace.

There is no doubt that there is a female factor at work in the marketplace. Melanie commented, "We are the fastest-growing segment in the US economy. Women don't even realize the power that we have. The way we think, the way we act, that's how the world is doing business." Here are some current statistics about the female factor. Globally, women reinvest 90 percent of their income in their families and communities, spending more earned income on food, healthcare, home improvement, and schooling for themselves and their children.[2] Women-owned businesses comprise up to 38 percent of all registered small businesses worldwide.[3] In the United States women hold half of America's wealth—estimated to be $11 trillion of a total $22 trillion by 2020.[4] Fleishman-Hillard Inc. estimates that women will control two-thirds of the consumer wealth in the United States over the next decade and be the beneficiaries of the largest transference of wealth in US history. Globally, half of all college students are now women. And in the United States and in the European Union, the majority are women (57 percent in the United States, 55 percent in the European Union).[5] Women dominate higher education in most developing countries. In the United States, women drive an estimated 70–80 percent of consumer spending with their purchasing power and influence.[6] Market estimates about their total purchasing prowess varies, ranging anywhere from $5 trillion to $15 trillion annually.[7] Since 1970, women have filled two new jobs for every one taken by a man.[8]

It is imperative that women's risk taking happens throughout our careers and results in women being well represented at all levels. It's good for us, and it's certainly also good for business, because it brings diversity in thought and perspectives to the table at all levels of the organization. Debbie spoke about this. "What excites me about this conversation is that there is so much reward in taking risks. Corporations need women who have the passion to continue to rise through the organization...So what I am passionate about is reaching women who do have that desire and intent, empowering them, emboldening them to be able to take the risk that can get them there, because corporate America will be stronger and more competitive when we can do that." The data backs up that having more women in management is good for business. From 2004 to 2008, the Fortune 500 companies with the most female board directors outperformed those with the least—by 16 percent on return on sales, and by 26 percent on return on invested capital.[9] Companies that had three or more women on boards for at least four of those years outperformed those with the lowest rates of female representation by 84 percent on return on sales, 60 percent on return on invested capital, and 46 percent on return on equity.[9] Companies with the highest share of women outperform companies with no women. In terms of return on equity, the top-quartile group (companies with 19–44 percent women board representation) exceeds by 41 percent the group with no women (22 vs. 15 percent), and in terms of operating results, the more gender-diverse companies exceed by 56 percent the group with no women (17 vs. 11 percent).[10]

Recently Wayne was asked to sit on the US Board of a group called the 30 Percent Club—an international group of Chairmen and business leaders that are committed to better gender balance at all levels of an organization through voluntary action. They focus on what they refer to as a pipeline of senior female talent. Wayne points out, "Business leadership is key. It helps promote diversity. In the United States, recognizing it is a different corporate governance framework, the aim from the start is better gender balance at senior management levels; as opposed to specific focus on a Board of Directors, which is what the Europeans are doing. We are looking at it a bit differently. This club doesn't believe in mandatory quotas being the right approach. They want meaningful, sustainable change. That is an important thing."

Recognize and address <u>cultural factors</u> that may influence the career risks women take.

In any conversation about women and risk taking in their careers it would be foolish not to acknowledge that cultural factors affect the appetite women have for taking risks and the support they get. The general perspective is that risk taking for women in the United States, the United Kingdom, and many European or other Western countries is relatively easier than it is for women in many other parts of the world.

Remember Yanyan, who spoke about women in China needing courage? Yanyan's first words to me when I interviewed her were, "I'm not a real typical Chinese girl." Losing her mother when she was thirteen years old laid a foundation of independence in her. At seventeen, while still at school, she started working part-time— according to Yanyan, this is atypical if you are from a well-off family in China. When she graduated from college, instead of following the traditional path of accepting a teaching position in a local middle school, she bucked the trend and pursued a higher degree in education in the city. Securing a full scholarship, she obtained her MA in Education and then veered off the beaten path again, choosing to resign her university teaching job to pursue her dream of starting her own language school.

Yanyan shared some insights into risk taking in her world, describing the typical life cycle for a typical Chinese girl: Finish high school by eighteen; if they have a chance to go to university, do it before they are twenty-three years old; pressure from parents to get married and have babies even prior to graduating; get a stable job; marry by twenty-four or twenty-five; and have babies one or two years later. She said usually if they don't have a baby then the family forces them to go see a doctor because Chinese women place so much importance on their babies. Yanyan commented on the consequences relative to risk taking in their careers, saying, "They ignore the job opportunities. Around thirty or thirty-two years old—I can tell because I am this age—most of my friends, they will feel kind of bored, or life has no

hope, this kind of thing. At forty years old it's too late to rebound...
My cousins and sisters, they feel now it is time to wait until they are
retired, they will say it is time to wait until you get old, because it is
too late to make some changes with your life. That is the typical
Chinese woman's life...If they know it's not too late they [will] have
more courage. I really hope they can change. They just need more
confidence."

Bindu has also always proudly charted her own course, taking
significant risks along the way. With a chuckle, she described herself
to me. "I am a bit of an oddity, if you will. I do exactly what I feel
like doing. When I was younger I would actually retort and say, 'So
what's your problem if I'm doing it?' I don't conform to any social
norms." Over the course of her career journey what she felt like doing
included being an entrepreneur at the age of twenty-three with her
husband of three years at the time. They dug into their savings and
sourced the additional finances they needed to found a computer
training institute. It included choosing to do an Executive MBA after
nearly twenty-one years of working and reaching a fairly senior
position; and in 2013, after nine years in the Employee Benefits
Outsourcing space at Aon-Hewitt, it included taking on a service
delivery role in the Asia-Pacific market—a business area with which
she had no prior experience.

Bindu felt particularly strongly about how the following two
cultural factors influence women's willingness to take more calculated
career risks in India: attitudes regarding women investing in their
ongoing career education, and the attitude towards what the women's
income contributes to the family. "A man looking for the same job
and a woman looking for the same job, the woman has to be a tad bit
more educated and a tad bit more hardworking than the man to prove
herself. So it may not be appropriate, it may not be fair, but that's how
it is. In my school the regular MBA program that people do after three
or four years of experience has 50 percent women candidates. When
the Executive MBA program is looked at, it's never gone beyond 10
percent of women." Bindu took issue with the fact that when she chose
to do the MBA program, a lot of her friends and relatives asked why

she was doing it instead of her husband, questioning why she needed to do an 'expensive' MBA program. She continued on, saying, "Most girls are brought up with, 'You need to know how to cook. You need to know how to manage a family. You need to nurture your children. So learn skills that will help you to do all of that. And by the way, if you are able to learn skills and go earn some money, it's some money, some job, supplemental income. It's not a career.'...In India most children—boys and girls—have very little freedom to pursue education of their choice. Parents insist on choosing the courses they take up and often girls are not allowed to pursue higher education. There are exceptions to this in urban cities, but even the really well educated woman's career is mostly viewed as a source of supplemental family income."

Vlada wants to succeed, she wants to progress in her career. Left as a single mom after her husband passed away, she chose to take a significant career risk—and in doing so, go against the norm of societal expectations in Russia. She took on the role of Executive Assistant to the global leader of BP's Lubricants business, which required her to move to the United Kingdom and spend significant periods of time traveling. Vlada said, "It's not only about women taking risk. It's also about their husbands and families supporting them to take this risk, or to take this risk with them...If you look into different cultures, the percentage of women able to risk will be absolutely different. If we speak about Russians, for example, it is more Asian-style orientation in terms of family. It is a big family orientation. It is very difficult for certain cultures to detach from this way of life. There is a normal picture which is associated with a woman being a mother, being a woman in the house, and so on. If you look at women of different nationalities, you will probably see how desperate Chinese, Indian, or Russian [women] are in this respect. I think it is because of this lack of ability to [take risk] for many years from generation to generation."

Appreciate and account for how risk taking in one's career fits in the broader <u>landscape of life.</u>

In the broader landscape of life you have to keep putting yourself out there to even have a shot at the risks and related opportunities. Erin, who continues to surpass her sales targets year after year, and who is being actively mentored by Leslie Lemenager to support Erin in her rise through the ranks, commented, "Not all risks will pan out. But you have to put yourself out there...Someone might have a vision for you that you don't have for yourself, or the position might not exist. But if you don't take risk in your career those opportunities are going to pass you by. It's important to be at the forefront of people's thoughts. So if they're thinking about a new position, they're thinking about you. If someone thinks of you as being a non-risk taker [and] if the role is not entirely developed, they won't even think to offer it to you."

In the broader landscape of life, no risk in your career or its consequences will last forever. Having the appetite to take calculated risks in one's career, knowing how to prepare for them, and having success with them leads to a more fulfilling and satisfying take on the landscape of life overall. Choose your risks and give them everything you've got for as long as they last. When you succeed in your risk taking it can remain a part of your landscape for a while. If you don't succeed you'll learn from the experience, you'll change things up and have another go at it. Melinda commented, "For me one thing I've always had in the back of my mind is nothing is ever permanent. If I make the wrong decision I can undo it, I can do something different."

In the broader landscape of life it's the amalgamation of risks you have taken over time that creates your risk-taking profile. Sometimes a big risk makes sense, and sometimes smaller baby steps are the right answer. Katie—who continues to reach out for and be given more and more responsibility in her organization—shared with me, "I am trying to work on taking smaller risks and putting myself out there while I am growing in my career. That way when I get to places where I can take larger risks I will be more comfortable with that. My delivery will be better when it's bigger risks if I've practiced it on smaller risks."

In the broader landscape of life taking a risk in your career is making a choice to thrive and not just to survive. You cannot realize your full potential if you're just about survival. Cathy views thriving in risk taking as having a growth experience with some real satisfaction and passion. She said, "My most heightened sense of energy is periods when I am daring a little and covering new ground. If you lock yourself in your comfort zone, you'll be comfortable. You survive, you may succeed, but you definitely won't thrive, because thriving embodies vitality and growth, and you won't have either one if you're always safe. You rob yourself of that experience."

Women and calculated risk taking in our careers is indeed an exciting and important conversation to have. The questions we need to answer next are: How do we move the needle? How do we shift ourselves and others on risk-taking continuums? What strategies and tactics can we use to get comfortable with and prepare ourselves to take more calculated risks and increase our success in our risk taking? That's what we are going to dive into next in Part II of *"Ready, Set...RISK!"*

Chapter 4 Notes:

1   Grey, Dr. Ronald J., and Gordon, Dr. George G. "Risk-taking managers: Who gets the top jobs?" *Management Review* 67 (1978): 8–13.

2   "Why Women? Why Now?" *US Department of State: Diplomacy in Action* (2010).

3   "Women Entrepreneurs and Access to Finance: Program Profiles from Around the World." *International Finance Corporation* (2010).

4   Tyrie, David. "What Women Can Teach Us About Money." *Spectrem Group* (2011).

5   Anderson, Doug. "Below the Topline Women's Growing Economic Power." *Nielsen* (2009).

6   Multiple sources, including *Boston Consulting Group*; Michael J. Silverstein, Michael J., and Sayre, Kate. *Women Want More.* Harper Collins, 2009; "A Guide to Womenomics." *The Economist* (2006); and Brennan, Bridget. *Why She Buys.* Crown Business, 2011

7   "US Women Control The Purse Strings." *Nielsen* (2013).

8   "A Guide to Womenomics." *The Economist* (2006).

9   "The Bottom Line: Corporate Performance and Women's Representation on Boards." *Catalyst* (2007).

10   "Women Matter: Making the Breakthrough." *McKinsey and Company* (2012).

PART TWO: *"Ready, Set..."*

Chapter 5: Believe in Yourself

I learned something important about myself very early in my life. I love to run fast, I love to compete, and I love to win! I still remember the day we did our first heats for sprinting. I was six years old and in grade one at Greenside Primary School in Johannesburg, South Africa. Track and field season started towards the end of winter, so there was still a chill and crispness in the air. They lined us up in some semblance of order along a line at one end of the field, told us to run as fast as we could to get to the people standing further down in the field, and then came the magic words, "On your marks...get set... go!" I was off, pumping my legs and arms as fast as I could, my bare feet slapping on the dry August grass, my dress flapping about (can you believe it—we ran in our dresses), focusing intensely on getting to the end point. A magical thing happened. I got there first! I still remember that realization creeping in. I got there first...and by a decent bit too, I might add!

In South Africa we were all assigned to houses (teams) in school. All kinds of interhouse competitions took place—athletics, rugby, field hockey, squash, drama, debating, etc. At my primary school the houses were named after explorers—Stanley, Livingstone, and Burton. I was in Stanley. Our house color was red (which by the way is my favorite color). Fast-forward to a few weeks later, and we were at the school inter-house competition. My first real competitive sprint race ever! Again I crossed the finishing line first, walking away with my first place cup. The wins continued, and I still remember receiving a cup that at the time seemed almost as big as me after winning multiple events one day. I was hooked. For the next twelve years of my life—throughout my school years—I was a very serious athletic competitor with the hundred-meter sprint being my best event.

It's time for you to take a deep breath and cast your mind backwards, all the way to when you were a little kid. Take another deep breath and keep that image in your head of yourself as a child. When we were kids anything was possible. There were no limits on our potential. Picture those childhood images of you doing anything and everything, no fear, no inhibitions, brave-hearted, and spirited. We just went for it with all our heart and energy and spirit, whatever the outcome might be. We took risks all the time without even knowing they were risks. Each and every time we took a risk—again, without even knowing it was a risk—we learned, we changed, we grew, and we loved it. We just did it, we just risked!

I took a risk running that first race. I had no idea what the outcome would be. I had no idea that the outcome even mattered, right? Winning or losing that first heat didn't matter. What mattered was that I gave it a try and took my best shot at it. Neither I nor anyone else knew the extent of my running capabilities until I actually ran that first heat. I didn't know what the best way was to run a race. I just ran, found out that I loved it, and was good at it, so I kept doing it, getting better and better at it all the time, with people encouraging me and coaching me and cheering me through all those years. Even to this day, I continue to run fast through life, or as I now like to say, I continue to risk through life. It's just the nature of what I am risking on and for that has changed. So now, instead of saying, "On Your Marks, Get Set, Go!" or "Ready, Set, Go!" you're far more likely to hear me yelling loudly and happily, *"Ready, Set…RISK!"*

For you—you wonderful, motivated, and engaged reader—it is imperative that I emphasize to you that to be successful in your calculated risk taking, fundamentally you have to believe in yourself and how much you are capable of. You have to believe anything is possible. You have to believe in all the potential you have. You have to create a mindset for yourself where you are reminded on a daily basis of all that potential; where in addition to having your kids/nieces/nephews' first-grade photographs on your desk, you also have your own first-grade photographs on your desk to remind you every day of your own potential.

In order to believe in and realize your potential, both you and others need to understand and recognize your value. Peg is a wonderful example of what can happen when value is recognized. She told me more of her story. "Early 2008 I was having a discussion with one of the guys on the Executive Committee. I was irritated at something he said. He was being dismissive of me. I said to him, 'Dammit, I'm a valuable Partner.' His response was, 'Well you could be a valuable Partner.' That was really the wake-up call to say, 'You're not valued here. You need to move someplace you're valued.' His snarky comment was probably one of the best things that somebody ever said to me, because it caught me up short and got me to really look at things and say, 'You're not happy here, you're not valued here, you need to move.' I changed firms, and I went to a firm that offered me a formula. They said if I billed greater than X, I would get 50 percent of what I billed. My attitude was, 'That's wonderful, but I haven't billed X in years.' I moved July 2008 and bankruptcy had been dead for a number of years. A couple of things happened. One—bankruptcy exploded. Two—a lot of the clients whom I got no credit for at the old firm, I was getting credit for at the new firm. A lot of clients moved over. I got to be tremendously busy. I also got a lot of variety. I was getting really challenged by both the type of the work and the quantity of the work."

Peg had finally tapped into her full potential and found a place where that potential and value was both recognized and appreciated. The positive impact of that manifested itself in a number of ways, starting with how happy she was. She told me about an observation her son made when he called her one day. "When I had been with the firm for about six months, my youngest son— who was fourteen then—called me. He said to me 'Mom, you know you always answer the phone the same way.' I said, 'Well, how's that?' He said, 'Well you always answer it 'Peg Anderson', with a cheerful uptick at the end.' So I said, 'What's your point?' He responded, 'At the old place you always answered it 'Peg Anderson', with a depressed drop-off tone.' I realized how happy the move had made me, but that was really great to have him crystallize the difference for me."

Sometimes it is hard to understand and recognize the extent of your own potential. We all experience doubts at some stage and have questions that linger in our heart and our head. But you cannot limit yourself in your risk taking by doubting your potential. Erin thinks this may indeed be her greatest limitation in her risk taking—

understanding her potential. She commented, "Oftentimes we second-guess ourselves or do something and then it lingers in our thoughts for days. 'Oh, did I do this the right way or did I do it the wrong way?' Either way, it's done—and you probably did it the best you could have done it given the environment and the circumstances of the situation. So I think it's realizing and understanding your potential." She also circled back to something that Leslie Lemenager had brought up earlier in the conversation, since I interviewed the two of them together. Erin recalled how Leslie had talked about the importance of having a partner that believes in your potential and that is fully supportive of you taking the risks that you do. Erin concurred with that, saying, "I think that that's so important. Having someone that is able to lift you up and take you to a new level that you didn't even know that you had [in you], having that support system. While you might have it internally, having it externally is just as important, whether it's a boyfriend or girlfriend or family or friend. That's really important because it will help you realize your potential and get over internal limitations that you set upon yourself."

Annette used to go into one-on-ones with her boss and say, "Maybe I didn't do that so well," or "Maybe I need to think about how I do this going forward," or "Am I ready for that particular opportunity?" Annette's boss told her she was limiting herself and holding herself back, saying to Annette, "You can take on the world, Annette, if you want or you try." Annette commented that the more she explored this the more aware she's become of the differences between men and women in their risk aversion. Acknowledging that she was generalizing, she said, "Women think about what could go wrong and what aspects of themselves are either just not 100 percent there or are inadequate for roles or promotions or developmental moves. They tend to hold themselves back and say, 'Maybe not yet,' or 'Give it a couple of years,' or whatever. Whereas men tend to overstate how good they are at things and willingly jump into roles they are not ready for. They'll make it work. The mindset is very different as they go in. I think this contributes to the fact that there are way fewer women at the top of organizations. Women are leaving themselves unfulfilled. It's this mindset that we seem to have grown up with [in] which women have more limiting beliefs than men. I think I used to fall into that category. That boss pointing that out to me really helped me think about this in a different way and think more consciously about, 'Am I holding myself back?' I do ask myself, 'Am I good enough?' So I've started to push myself more."

Taking risks and being successful in your risk taking requires a willingness to stretch yourself and to change. That's how you'll realize your full potential. Maureen spoke about asking and answering for oneself the questions, "Are you willing to put in the work that is going to be necessary to change what you've known? Are you really ready to take this up to the next level for yourself?" If you believe in your potential—if the answer to those questions is "Yes!"—then taking the calculated risk is a smart thing to do. Roger spoke about it in terms of stretching yourself. "Understand what you want as an individual and what willingness or openness you have to stretch and risk. When I talk about risk I talk about stretch. When I look at opportunities within my career, I look at a role and say, 'How much stretch is in that role versus where I am currently?' If a role is 100 percent stretch, chances are if I were going to go in and do it, it would probably take me a long time to become competent or even highly efficient." He contrasted that with if he were to move into a role where there is something like 60–70 percent stretch and is in an area where he already has some expertise—how much more successful he could be at realizing his potential in that situation. So if you believe in your potential, if you know your stretch tolerance and that matches with the risk at hand, then taking a calculated risk is a smart thing to do.

In the June 2014 issue of the *Harvard Business Review* there was a superb article titled "21st Century Talent Spotting" by Claudio Fernández-Aráoz in which he spoke about how organizations need to move away from their past models and philosophies of emphasizing "competencies" when developing and hiring talent, and instead move towards focusing on potential—"the ability to adapt to ever-changing business environments and grow into challenging new roles."[1] I literally got goose bumps reading this article. Why did the article resonate so strongly with me? Because in it he calls out five indicators of potential he and colleagues identified in some research they conducted: the right kind of motivation, curiosity, insight, engagement, and determination. Take a look at how they described each of those indicators in the article:

> *"The right kind of motivation:* A fierce commitment to excel in the pursuit of unselfish goals. High potentials have great ambition and want to leave their mark, but they also aspire to big, collective goals, show deep personal humility, and invest in getting better at everything they do."[1]

> *"Curiosity:* A penchant for seeking out new experiences, knowledge, and candid feedback, and an openness to learning and change"[1]

> *"Insight:* The ability to gather and make sense of information that suggests new possibilities"[1]

> *"Engagement:* A knack for using emotion and logic to communicate a persuasive vision and connect with people"[1]

> *"Determination:* The wherewithal to fight for difficult goals despite challenges, and to bounce back from adversity"[1]

I would certainly also use these terms to describe someone who is comfortable with and has success with taking calculated risks. If you look at people whom you know are good at taking calculated risks and turning them into opportunity, they are highly motivated and invariably driven by a dedicated purpose and focus that keeps them on their path, even when the going gets tough and they encounter obstacles. They are curious—seeking out the data and knowledge and information they need to make informed decisions as they continue down their risk-taking and opportunity-seeking path. They display insight and use that to build confidence with others who are risking on or with or for them. They are highly engaged, skilled at communicating and getting others on board with why the risk is worth taking, what the opportunity will yield, what the journey will look like, and getting people to stick with it when challenges are encountered. They do not give up; they persevere and are extremely determined. Sure, there are some nuanced differences in how you would state these for risk takers versus high potentials, but there is also a huge amount of overlap.

Every single one of you reading this book has great potential. I know you do. You know you do. When you are focused on the risks that are right for you, you will be driven by the right kind of motivation; you will exude curiosity and insight and engagement and determination. In taking calculated risks, you will then learn new skills. Those new skills are what will put you in a marvelous position to adapt and grow into increasingly complex roles and environments in your organization. What makes someone successful in a particular role today might not be the same tomorrow if the competitive environment changes, or business strategy changes, or the team makeup is different. Those are the kinds of resources organizations want to find, recruit, and retain to let their organization be the best it can be—resources that can adapt and grow. So if you believe in your potential, if you let that belief in your potential propel you and drive you, then taking a calculated risk is a smart thing to do and will place you in a position where you are considered for and placed into roles that truly leverage your potential to maximum effect.

On a chilly Tuesday afternoon I stepped into the Lincolnwood operations facility of Food For Thought. The comforting aroma of freshly cooked food assailed my sense of smell. The cozy warmth that comes from ovens on the go warmed me up immediately as I stood in the reception area. It was a good thing I had already eaten lunch before I came to interview the CEO and cofounder, Nancy Sharp. Nancy greeted me with a hug. After I dropped my bag and laptop off in her office, she gave me a tour of the Food For Thought operations (the food being prepared looked scrumptious), and then we settled down for the interview.

Nancy opened up to me right away. "It's the very words we use that box us into limited thinking. I think the word risk is a limiting word. I never look at things as being risky. I look at everything that walks into my life as being an opportunity. If you want something in life then find the opportunity in it, compare the opportunity along the way, and make good choices for yourself at all levels…Most people who are successful are not risk takers; they are opportunists. They see an opportunity and they want data to confirm the opportunity, they make a decision on the opportunity, and then they look at the time schedule in which the opportunity can come to fruition. Then it's an opportunity. It's not a risk. I let go of my belief system that I couldn't do something. As you grow up you have these belief systems—'Wow I am only this smart compared to other people.' Lose that. You have all these voices in your ear…your last boss or your mother or your uncle or your husband or whomever, saying 'That's risky,' or 'You shouldn't do that,' or 'You don't know enough.' They are telling you the things that aren't possible. They aren't telling you, 'I'm so proud of you. Continue on your path. Go look for new opportunities.' You begin to own other people's perception of their own fear. You start to fear it yourself, and then you come up with all these notions of what you couldn't do, shouldn't do, can't do. Until you let go of what you can't do, can you open your mind to what you can do?"

I loved that last statement of hers, "Until you let go of what you can't do, can you open your mind to what you can do?" When you fully believe in your potential—which you must—you will let go of what you can't do, you will open your mind to and embrace what you can do, and you will be willing to take more calculated risks and turn them into opportunity for yourself and for others. To be successful in your calculated risk taking you have to believe in your potential and how much you are capable of. You have to believe anything is possible. You have to believe in yourself.

Chapter 5 Notes

1   Fernández-Aráoz, Claudio. "21st Century Talent Spotting." *Harvard Business Review* (June 2014): 49–52.

Chapter 6: Know Yourself

To put yourself in the best position to open your mind to and embrace what you can do, ask and answer the following three questions for yourself:

One: **Do I know what my leading strengths are?**

Two: **Do I have reliable and effective feedback
        mechanisms in place?**

Three: **Have I acknowledged my challenge points?**

These factors provide a strong foundation to ensure that you really know yourself. In knowing yourself you can prepare for and conduct your calculated risk taking in a manner that maximizes your chances for success.

One: Do I know what my leading strengths are?

Research has shown repeatedly that people have much more potential for growth when they invest in developing and building on their strengths instead of relentlessly trying to eliminate their deficiencies. In Tom Rath's book *StrengthsFinder 2.0* he points out that Gallup studies have shown that people who do have the opportunity to focus on their strengths every day are six times as likely to be engaged in their jobs, and that having a manager who focuses on your strengths brings the chances of you being actively disengaged down to 1 percent.[1] Whenever you take a risk in your career, you will need to be extremely engaged with all aspects of that risk, so leveraging your core strengths is crucial in your risk taking. When it comes to risk taking, people who are leveraging their strengths to maximum effect are more likely to push themselves into taking risks and to be successful in those risks and yield the desired benefit, both personally and organizationally.

Karen shares my passion for this aspect of preparing for risk taking, commenting, "It starts off with knowing yourself. There's a variety of assessments out there. Go through those at several points in your career to really understand what's working for you and what will work for you. Once you understand that, it gives you a sense of confidence that underpins the ability to take risks. It helps you understand what you'll be successful at, and that success can be experienced in a variety of environments if you know the source of your best contribution, how you best show up."

In Karen's role as head of Talent Management at Zurich North America she is well versed in the array of tools available. She and I are both fans of *StrengthsFinder 2.0* and recommend it, particularly in terms of how easy it is to access it and source materials that help you understand how to apply it to yourself. Karen also recommends the Hogan inventories. At Zurich North America they use a version of Hogan that has three inventories—your strengths, your values (how do your values best align to an organizational culture), and your derailments. Karen commented on how the derailments inventory is particularly useful in the context of the stress that occurs when you take a risk. "If you're under stress—depending on how susceptible you are to stress—there is the potential of some derailing behaviors showing up. So you've spent all this time establishing credibility and using your strengths to be a contributor in a consistent way, and suddenly, 'Who is this? What have you done with the person that we know?' That can undermine your credibility." She also commented on the power of 360 feedback surveys, Myers-Briggs Type Indicator®, True Colors®, and DiSC®. "All of those tools are excellent and accessible for getting that baseline understanding of where you might steer things and what you might be best suited to. If you are grounded with that kind of information, you can have that to inform your choices going forward. If you're playing to your strengths, that builds on the probability of you being successful, that feedback gives you additional confidence, [and that] confidence gives you the ability to make riskier choices that in essence will broaden what you are able to do. The starting point is you understanding how you can best show up."

There is no right time or best time to take one of these assessments. Any time is a good time because it will help you be at your best and give you continued confidence in your risk taking. In my last few years at Deloitte I would at times get extremely frustrated when I asked for but was not given the opportunity to work on projects that were more strategic in nature than the complex technology implementation projects I was leading up for clients. I still remember more than one person saying to me, "You're not strategic." That drove me crazy, because I absolutely believed I was strategic, and that, given the right opportunities, I would excel in the strategy arena. Since I felt strongly that working with clients on issues of a more strategic nature was part of my journey to realize my full potential and make my biggest contributions, the constant pushback and those opportunities never coming to fruition was one of the factors that contributed to my decision to leave Deloitte. Fast forward to 2012, when I started to work on my second company focused on development and advancement of women in the workplace. I was being as strategic as strategic could get: coming up with bold new innovative ideas and business plans and linking them to challenges and opportunities corporations are facing in the areas of talent management, multicultural diversity and inclusion; pitching programs to corporations; building excitement around me as I went about building the second business; and adapting the strategy as things evolved.

I still remember the day I took the *StrengthsFinder 2.0* assessment. I sat in my home office at my desk that faces east over the prairie conservancy, the sun shone in through the blinds, and I clicked away at the questions, eager to see what the report would provide me with in terms of insights. When I got the report and reviewed it, I yelled out loud, "I'm strategic! I'm strategic!" There it was, right up there amongst my top five leading strengths—strategic! It's not that I needed a piece of paper to tell me what I always knew in my gut. However, it did provide me with a validation, and it did further bolster my confidence that I was indeed—more so than ever before—

tapping into the sources of my best contributions, more fully realizing my potential, and showing up in my best way—and that I should indeed continue to trust in myself and my vision and continue to take the risks I was taking with this whole new venture.

If you haven't already invested in identifying your leading strengths, in figuring out how you best show up, invest some time and some money in taking one of these assessments and debriefing the results with someone who is skilled and knowledgeable in how to internalize the results and use them to maximum benefit for yourself. It will make a marked difference in your willingness, ability, and success with taking more risks in your career and turning them into opportunity.

Two: Do I have reliable and effective feedback mechanisms in place?

The second key component to knowing yourself and becoming more effective with your risk taking is the tried and trusted, age-old gift of feedback. In this case I am not talking about the structured, 360-survey type feedback that Karen spoke about. This is the formal and informal feedback you seek out for yourself in a one-on-one type of setting. The advice you get and what you learn is invaluable in preparing yourself for more effective risk taking. Sometimes the feedback may even steer you towards something you might not otherwise have considered. Here are five fabulous factors you should incorporate into your approach to getting feedback that will serve you well in your risk taking: get instant and timely feedback; get honest and unfiltered feedback; be willing to ask questions; obtain multigenerational perspectives; and give people permission to reject you.

When you take risks in your career, **getting instant and timely feedback** from people who are willing to speak their mind is critical as you map out your next steps in your journey. Get the feedback before you make your next key decision or take your next step, not after the fact. Bindu commented, "Feedback is critical to success, risky, not risky, whatever it is. Feedback helps you to get new ideas, test your own ideas, and keep your feet on the ground. The minute you stop getting or soliciting feedback, you are bound to make a mistake. I am a huge believer in receiving feedback and equally in giving feedback. I give instant feedback. It's never only at the time of the appraisal. Every one-on-one conversation always closes with feedback."

When you're taking risks it is extremely tempting to only hear from and listen to those that are telling you what you want to hear. It's hard enough to take risks as it is. It can become quite draining when you have to spend time talking about what's not working or process what other people are saying that may not align with your vision. Many people won't want to give you that honest and unfiltered feedback—because they don't want to burst your bubble, or because they don't feel comfortable doing so, or for other reasons. But when people say feedback is a gift, it is absolutely true. So make sure you are **getting honest and unfiltered feedback** from trusted sources so you can decrease your exposure.

Cathy spoke about how important it is to identify people with whom you have already established trusted relationships, and who are willing to give you honest and unfiltered feedback along the way. She used the example of her taking on the new Chief People Officer role at BDO. She doesn't necessarily know where people are coming from as they respond to her direction, initiatives, and plans. She's taking risks as she explores the path forward, and she needs honest and unfiltered feedback. Are they trying to build relationships with her so they aren't giving her straight feedback, or are her strategy and ideas truly hitting the mark? She told me, "So I went to this person who I already have a completely established and trusting relationship with. I said, 'Here is what I need from you if you are willing. Will you be the mirror? I need an absolute undistorted mirror of, 'That was good, that's not working, that didn't resonate well, this is what you are saying, and this is the way that is perceived.' I need somebody to give that to me absolutely unfiltered, without any agenda or concern about the effects on them." She continued, "This person is providing me with an incredible service. What can be better than that? You know when you've got something genuine with people. I am not sure I have the secret recipe for how you get to this. There is a level that goes past candor. There is almost a level of vulnerability necessary to get to a really authentic interchange with people, and then you know you've got each other."

You must be willing to ask questions when taking risks. If you are not the type of person who asks questions, it's going to set you back in your success with your risk taking. Risk takers can't let worries about how other people might view your knowledge base or capabilities stop you from asking a question. You need to have enough confidence in yourself and in what you are doing that you can recognize that, if you have that question, somebody else probably has it in their mind too. Have enough confidence in your own intellect to realize you are not being ridiculous if you don't know that thing you are asking about. It's your risk; so you may as well be the one to ask the question. That shows insight and foresight. If you wait to ask it until it's too late, or somebody else asks it, that just shows hindsight. Just organize your thoughts to ask what you need to know in the right sequence, so you are learning in an orderly way that can support you in your risk taking. People appreciate that. Sue stressed, "It's OK not to know. It's OK to learn. I've never had a problem saying to somebody, 'I don't understand. Can you let me know? That doesn't make sense to me. Can you put that in a different way?' Don't be afraid to say, 'I don't know.' Make sure you go out and find out what the answer is."

You need to get feedback from people who think differently than you do to help you be successful in your risk taking. One great way to do that and decrease your risk exposure is to obtain multigenerational perspectives. Jan shared the story of a wonderful lady—now deceased—who was a granddaughter of Amelia Earhart, and who took Jan under her wing and counseled her in her risk taking. "This woman lived in a 14,000-square-foot home. She'd invite me over for tea, and I'd go. She'd give me all this advice. There's nothing better than listening to the advice of someone who's been through something, have it be sound advice, and give you that little edge that you might need next week." Toni concurred that there's wisdom to be learned from all generations when it comes to taking risks. She maintains she's learned as much from her mother and grandmothers as she has from her eleven-year-old daughter, saying, "She can sometimes cut through the forest and help me see the trees way better than anybody else because she has a different perspective on life. She's at a different stage. She just sees it differently than I do, and she always will see it differently. Even when she's in her twenties and I'm in a different stage in my life, she'll still be wise and an influence to me."

Last but not least, part of getting feedback when taking risks is to **give people permission to reject you.** Do not let fear of rejection stop you from taking a risk and asking for something. Melinda is someone who is not fearful of being rejected. She spoke about the pattern she often sees with people who say, "Oh, I'm not going to ask for that job, because I may not get it. They may think I'm ridiculous for asking, because who am I to ask for that because I've never been head of HR before? They are just going to think this is silly. They are just going to say no. I don't even know what got into me." She said, "You see that pattern with people. I think that's why they perceive sometimes that when you do what you want or you ask for what you want, that you are taking a risk. But don't be afraid of rejection. Give people permission to reject you. Because it's the only time you're really going to be able to explore doing something new and different."

When I launched the gen-xyb™ High Tea program to corporations in Chicago, I was doing something no one else had done before. I was turning over rocks and breaking new ground. I had to give myself permission to be rejected. I had to give people permission to reject me and my ideas. I didn't tell them that, of course, but mentally and emotionally I had to do that. If I didn't, I would have wanted to give up every time someone said no to me. Many companies said yes, and that kept me moving forward, but every no could have been an invitation to fold and give up. But by giving myself permission to be rejected, and mentally and emotionally giving others permission to reject me and my ideas, the no's just became part of my risk-taking journey. Every no became a feedback opportunity to learn why they were saying no, so I could build a case to try and shift them to a yes. Giving people permission to reject you will ultimately help you be more successful in your calculated risk taking.

Three: Have I acknowledged my challenge points?

The third key aspect of knowing yourself is to know what I call your "challenge points." Your challenge points are characteristics of yours that, if not monitored and managed, can trip you up in your risk taking. On the one hand they are characteristics you display that often serve you well, that are part of who you are and what you are known for, perhaps even tying to one or more of your strengths. But when taking risks they can become an Achilles heel or a double-edged sword, sometimes looming so large that they overshadow other strengths of yours that need to prevail front and center in order for you to be successful with the risk you are taking on.

Let me share with you a personal example about myself. I excel at turning strategy, ideas, and talk into actionable plans and reality. I love to make a plan and execute in accordance with the plan. I am extremely good at keeping track of multiple moving parts in those plans for highly complex situations and keeping the ship moving forward. I love checking the boxes and moving on to the next thing. I get antsy when things are all over the place and lack any semblance of order or structure. I don't mind too much if things need to change, but in my mind they should change against a baseline plan, and they should result in a new plan that is in turn actively monitored and managed against. Furthermore, if I take something on, it is going to get done and it is going to get done well. Not surprisingly these characteristics tie in wonderfully with aspects of three of my five leading strengths that were identified in my *StrengthsFinder 2.0* report—Achiever, Focus, and Activator. These characteristics and other aspects of those three strengths have been very good to me over the years.

What I recognized when I took the *StrengthsFinder 2.0* assessment and reflected back is that these very leading strengths of mine had also become my challenge points at Deloitte. The very things that had helped me be extremely successful in my career there also overshadowed two of my other leading strengths that were crucial in my efforts to take risks and do different things—be they at Deloitte or elsewhere. No wonder things played out they way they did. My entire reputation at Deloitte was built on me being an excellent Project Manager. I was so wrapped up in the kind of work that played to three of my leading strengths—Achiever and Focus and Activator—that there was no time or opportunity to let my other leading strengths—Strategic and Maximizer—get their share of the spotlight. You could give me the toughest, most complicated, most budget-constrained project with deadlines that would make anyone sick, and I would manage it to successful completion on time and within budget. I kept on getting those types of projects to execute because I was so good at them. So good at it, in fact, that even though I believed I had strategy-oriented talents and skills, no one could see that what I was doing and the projects I was leading didn't call for those skills. They called for Achiever and Focus and Activator strengths. No wonder no one else thought I was strategic. In reality, though, I am. That has been proven by what has transpired since I left Deloitte. But in order to realize my full potential, I had to acknowledge this combination of factors as one of my challenge points and actively manage it to be successful in my risk taking.

There are many challenge points that I have covered in my discussions, but three come up time and time again that across the board are felt to be key inhibitors to women taking risks in their careers. We will cover these three in the rest of this chapter. I am sure many of you will identify with at least one of them and perhaps even all three. Certainly there are many more. I encourage all of you to identify your own challenge points and manage them accordingly to increase your success with your risk taking.

Challenge point: Taking responsibility for everything that is put in front of you

This is about taking on too much, saying "yes" to everything that comes your way, ending up with a plate of responsibilities that is overloaded, and pulling your attention away from where it should be focused as you navigate your risk.

"I tend to take responsibility for anything that is put in front of me. It's just easier to do it all yourself so you end up working all the time. But it's not the best thing for the company because you're not empowering people. You're certainly not sharing thought, and it can be detrimental to your health." Those words are from Jan, who shared an example of how when she hired a Vice President of Operations she struggled with stepping back, and that it took a few years for her to fully let the new hire do the job she had been hired to do. Jan elaborated on how letting go of certain responsibilities and delegating to the new VP ultimately benefited both herself and the company overall by freeing up her time to manage the risks associated with the next phase of growth for her company. Mukta also shared her sentiments on this challenge point. "I can take on too much, because I like to achieve things. It doesn't mean I can't do it, but something has to give. What always gives is my own time...So knowing how much I can extend myself can sometimes be tricky because I want to do so much and I am enthusiastic. I know I can do it. But it doesn't always mean I have the time to do it."

Spreading yourself too thin is not a good strategy to achieve success in your risk taking. How can you possibly be comfortable taking risk in your career and managing risk in your career if you are juggling too many balls in the first place, or if you can't get things done the way you want to because you have too much that you are trying to handle? Furthermore, if you say yes to everything, then when that risky but exciting opportunity comes along that you really want, you may not have the capacity to take it on. Even worse, others may not consider you as a candidate for it because they feel you are too overloaded. So stop taking responsibility for everything that is put in front of you. You need to work on two tactics to help you in this arena: get comfortable with saying "no," and work on delegating to others. Before you agree to take on the next thing that is put in front of you, make sure you understand and accept how it will impact the outcome of any career risk you are currently managing or that you want to take. If it doesn't have a positive impact, decline it or get rid of it, and don't feel bad on either count. You have to be extremely disciplined with prioritizing how you use your precious time if you are going to be effective at taking risks in your career.

Challenge point: Needing to know everything before moving forward

Yes, you want to do a reasonable degree of analysis and have some good data to help you make decisions about the career risks you will or will not take. But at some point as you expand your experience base you have to learn to go with your intuition, to trust your gut. You do not need to know everything before you step forward into the risk. Take a step back and look more holistically at the situation. Ask yourself questions such as: How do I feel about the situation? If it involves working with people, how do I feel about working with those people? How do I feel about that company's products and that company's brand? Is this something I am going to have fun with and be proud to be associated with? Do I have a good feeling about it, and do I think it's going to work out or not?

Katie described her point of view on this challenge point, saying it's about "...confidence and delivery and trusting in your gut. Not feeling like you have to know all the information. As long as you know some of the information and that what you are pulling from is solid, while you may not have all the information you need if you trust your gut, then you should be confident in the risks you are recommending to take." She acknowledged she has work to do as it relates to this challenge point. "I am very detail oriented. Not having all the details tends to make me less comfortable with taking risks. When you take a risk you generally have less control. I like knowing the details, and knowing I have control over the project I am working on, or whatever risk I am taking. If you are taking a risk, you have less control. I don't feel comfortable when I don't have control over all the information."

At one of the 2014 gen-xyb™ High Tea sessions, a guest panelist shared a decision-making framework he had heard about that talks about the elephant and the rider as the decision metaphor. The elephant is the unconscious and the rider is the conscious. When a person is up on the elephant, they are guiding the elephant, but ultimately the elephant is going to do what the elephant wants to do. You have to recognize there is an elephant inside each of us that is the deeper, contemplative part of ourselves, and that is ultimately what is going to make the decision about the risk at hand. We don't want to be totally irrational and totally intuitive, so we have to think about the analytical part of it—but don't be afraid to be in touch with deeper feelings about your situation and to go with your gut instinct on the career risk.

Challenge point: Wanting to be perfect at all that you do

If you've done it before and know exactly how to do it, it's not a risk. Taking a risk in your career inherently implies there is an element of the unknown in the journey that lies ahead of you, a lot of learning to be done, and that most likely you're not going to get it all right all the time. To be successful in taking risks in your career requires you to let go of wanting to be perfect in everything that you do. Stop striving for perfection.

Debbie commented, "I think it's typical of many women in business—we want to do things to 100 percent perfection. We don't want to fall short of anyone else's expectations or of our own. Early in my career when I was offered a new opportunity I'd think, 'I'm not equipped to do this thing perfectly, and I want to do it perfectly right away.' Then I'd compare myself to others. As I grew and learned, I realized it isn't about how others might do this job or how qualified someone else might be. It was about me focusing on what I bring to the role and re-grounding myself on the things I know are important and that work."

Sue also said that she won't accept mediocrity in herself, that she wants to excel at everything she does. "But," she pointed out, "sometimes with taking risk you can't have everything to the level that you want to have it. You have all these personal pressures you put on yourself, when really you need to focus on what you want to achieve— what's your goal at the end of it? Step back; be very honest with yourself. You have to accept that you're not going to tick every box every time. You need to prioritize which boxes are the most important.

It's a negotiation factor—negotiate what you really want to achieve from this and what you're going to let go [of]."

Nancy Mueller made the point that other people aren't expecting you to be perfect, irrespective of whether you are male or female. She posed a powerful but simple question. "So why would you expect that of yourself?" She then proceeded to share a story with me. "Another key turning point in my career was shortly after I was named Chief Actuary. That role was on the Executive team, and it was a direct report to the CEO. I was a mother of young children at the time. There weren't a lot of women on the Executive team. Most of the [Executive team] members—their children were grown. I was balancing two young kids, and Frank Patalano [Chief Operating Officer at Zurich North America at the time] was a mentor, and he saw the stress I was under. He came to me and said, 'You know, Nancy, you have to decide. You can't be perfect. You can't be the perfect executive, the perfect wife, the perfect mother, the perfect friend, the perfect daughter. That's too much for anyone. You have to decide where you're going to focus and when you're going to focus, but you can't always be perfect.' " Frank saw that Nancy was holding herself up to trying to do it all perfectly. Frank helped her realize that nobody can do that, that she needed to give herself leeway, because no one else had that expectation of perfection. She summed it up by saying that what's really important when you take a risk and assume a new role in your career, or even if you've been in a role for a while, is being able to match expectations of what you expect of yourself and what the people around you expect of you.

Chapter 6 Notes

1   Rath, Tom. *StrengthsFinder 2.0*. Gallup Press, 2007: iii–iv.

Chapter 7: The Power of Your Story

Your story is a powerful part of your tool kit for risk taking. It portrays important characteristics about you that are relevant to your risk taking, and it provides context for the motivation that lies behind your risk taking. Far more powerful than an essay of your entire life history is your "book of short stories"; that is, your series of vignettes that you pick and choose from based on what is most relevant for you to communicate in the situation at hand. The power of your story is a key component in what gets others to a place where they are willing and excited to take a risk on you, or with you, or for you. Figuring out your stories and how to tell them in a powerful way is a process you need to work your way through on an ongoing basis. Fundamentally, your story work is never done. It will always be evolving if your life and career and risk taking are evolving.

Like Erin, Katie is another young, rising star, the epitome of the Millennials that are the future female leaders in the workplace. These young women are engaging, courageous, fearless, motivated, and inspired, starting to flex their risk-taking muscles, and eager to stretch themselves early and often. After graduation Katie headed to Chicago to look for a job in event planning in the nonprofit arena. A savvy social media user, she followed one of her target prospective employers and their CEO on Twitter and exchanged a couple of tweets with the CEO. Her Twitter bio said she was looking for an event-planning job in Chicago. The CEO reached out to her via Twitter, asked if she was still looking for a job, and asked for her resume. A phone interview with the Director of HR followed. Then, in a flash of inspiration and genius, Katie decided that instead of sending a thank-you note, she was going to take a risk and do something out of the ordinary. Katie told me her story about the size-ten shoes.

"After the phone interview was when I put the shoes together. One was for the Director of HR, who I had spoken with on the phone interview, and the other for the CEO, who I had interacted with via Twitter. Each size-ten shoe was accompanied by a note that said something along the lines of, 'I am ready to take the next step in my career at Event 360.'...I actually took it to their front desk. I was standing there in one of those buildings where you have to get access to the elevator. I was standing there with two shoes, talking to the elevator attendant and trying to explain that I had to take up a pair of shoes because I'd had a phone interview. They called the office manager, who rang me up. I gave them to her and explained who they were for and thanked her and left. It was very nerve wracking. The person I gave them to was very surprised that I was handing her a giant pair of shoes, and said thank you to me. I hoped that she would deliver them to the people that they were supposed to go to. They did get delivered to the right people, and they did like them, and that's what got me the in-person interview. They hadn't seen anything like that before. The Twitter connection helped too, because they were looking for someone to do something on social media. But it also showed that I was a fit within their culture, that I was creative and thought outside of the box, which was what I needed for that role. Taking that risk led to being able to talk to everyone face to face." Katie continues to work at Event 360. She has now been there over two years and continues to have great success within the company—being given significantly expanded roles and responsibilities in relatively short timeframes.

This story does a far better job of telling us so much about Katie— the type of person she is, what she stands for, how she thinks and operates—than any laundry list of where she went to school, what she studied, and her history of responsibilities at her job. Clearly this story portrays Katie in a calculated risk-taking capacity. In addition, because of what we learn about Katie in the story, it also helps us decide in what type of context we would be willing to take a risk on Katie, or for Katie, or with Katie. That's the power of Katie's story in the context of risk taking.

Good stories are crucial in the context of your risk taking because they:

- Make you memorable

- Get people to understand your motives for taking risk, obtain a sense of your character, and believe in your capabilities to be successful in your risk taking

- Enable you to enlist supporters to and make effective use of your contacts by helping them understand how their experience, knowledge, and network have relevance and can be of assistance as you navigate risk

- Make others want to help you in your risk taking because they are inspired by you, because you made them care, because you gained their trust and confidence, and now they feel vested in your success

- Help you believe in yourself, reassure you that your chosen path makes sense, and keep you motivated when the going gets tough as you navigate through risk

We will cover three sets of pointers in the rest of this chapter to help you develop your own authentic stories to use in the context of your risk taking: decide what type of story you are telling; include the fundamental components for any good story; make it real—be uniquely and authentically you.

Decide what type of story you are telling.

For people to believe in your motivation and abilities with risk taking, you need to be able to talk about a variety of components, such as what inspired you to take a risk; what experiences in your life have contributed to your readiness to risk; how you've survived challenges in the past; what you've done when things haven't gone as planned; how you've stayed true to your core values during the course of your risk taking; and how you turned a negative into a positive.

You need to have stories that illustrate how you have leveraged your leading strengths and overcome your challenge points while taking risks in your career. You need to have stories that showcase your communication skills and your ability to get others on board with you in your risk taking. Think long and hard about your career and life history, and build your book of short stories. When told with energy, passion, confidence, and real humility, your stories are part of your risk-taking tool kit. Here are some wonderful examples:

Melanie founded Exclusive Interim Properties, which later merged with four other companies to form BridgeStreet Worldwide. She told me her story about what inspired her to take the risk and found the company. She and her husband had just moved to New York City with their two little children. They both had high-powered jobs—Melanie with IBM and her husband with Merrill Lynch. "We needed somewhere to live. What was really interesting is I could not find short-term housing. No one offered anything less than a year. I wanted something for two to three months. I did what any intelligent woman would do—we moved into the Plaza Hotel!...That was the 'aha' moment." Melanie couldn't believe that in the big city of New York there was nothing short term. That gave her the seed vision for a business. When they moved to Baltimore, Maryland, two years later and yet again ended up living in a hotel for three months, she decided to do the due diligence and see if there was a business model for short-term accommodations that could be successful. Seven months later she concluded there was one, and she resigned from IBM to open up shop—a business that provided short-term accommodations for relocated executives.

She told me another story, this one about how she first got started, and how the company grew. "I started with my guest house. I ran an ad—Executive Rental, complete with linens, china, just bring your toothbrush, with maid service. I rented it within twenty-four hours. I remember this clearly—he was a big executive, and he said, 'When will the maid start?' I couldn't get maid service at that point. So guess who was the maid? Me! He would go to work and I would make sure the cottage was gorgeous. Then of course I hired my whole team. We did short-term accommodations for relocated executives, for professional sports— for example the Baltimore Ravens. We did twenty-three motion pictures from Hollywood. We did temporary assignments, we had burn-down families, and we had divorce cases. I ended up with 650 furnished properties with a Washington office and a Baltimore office. Then we did a roll-up in 1997. Four of us got together that provided this service around the United States, and we formed BridgeStreet Worldwide. It's now one of the largest in the world. We merged under one umbrella and did an IPO."

Kim's story of the tough situation she was in when she got promoted to Managing Director gave us direct insight as to how she manages her career risk. Remember Maureen's story of how she left Lettuce Entertain You and then they approached her to come back, which she did? That's a story that speaks volumes about Maureen's strengths in her core skill sets as well as how she builds and maintains relationships during the course of her risk taking. Janet and Karen told me stories about time they spent living and working in Russia. Yanyan, Bindu, Sue, Annette, Erin, and Vlada all shared stories with me in a way that clearly portrayed their global and cultural insights. When I hear stories that portray global experience and multicultural awareness, it imbues confidence in me that those people will be able to navigate multicultural risk. You need all types of stories in your inventory. Then you start to read into a situation regarding which one to share when.

Include the fundamental components for any good story.

I used to collect comic books—specifically *Catwoman* and *Batman*. Catwoman is still my favorite comic book character. On a related note, I enjoy some of the comic genre movies. Recently I watched the movie *Superman Returns*. Kevin Spacey is great in the Lex Luthor role. I loved the movie! It had all the classic elements of a great story: good and evil characters, plot, connections, and emotion. Whether it's a childhood fairytale, the alternate world of comics, or your favorite fiction or nonfiction story or movie, those elements remain the quintessential components of a great story. Read any reference book on the subject of storytelling and that's what they talk about in some variation or another: good and evil characters, plot, connections, and emotion. When it comes to your stories that you have ready to share in the context of your risk taking, you need all of those components, plus one more: maintaining a positive tone throughout, even when you are dealing with a topic that could be viewed as potentially negative in nature. In general people don't like to risk with people that come across as negative. You have to instill confidence and positivity at every turn when it comes to risk taking.

For a wonderful story that illustrates these five components, let's join Diane on the golf course back in her caddying days. Diane told me that reactions were mixed to having girl caddies. Some of the men welcomed them, some liked having little thirteen-year-old girls at their beck and call, and some would specifically state that they didn't want a girl caddy. Lots of the men were very motivating. They asked the girls about their future, about college and career plans, and gave them advice about relationships and networking. Many of the men were impressed that a young girl would carry a bag for four and a half hours. They were uplifted by it, would encourage and push the girl caddies in a positive way, and reward them with a generous tip on top of the base pay. The girl caddies learned a lot of lessons about how to deal with men and boys across the board. They moved up the caddy ranks, learning a variation of office politics in the caddyshack as they dealt with the politics of who got what caddy number, who made the caddy assignments to the golfers, and the consequences of doing something wrong—the caddy master (an Irish fellow) would say "Hit the bricks," and send the caddy home for the day.

Diane told me one of her landmark caddying stories, one that in my mind encapsulates so much about Diane as a risk taker. She was caddying for a male club member who was being very rude and making sexist comments all the way through the round—far worse than the typical innuendoes the girl caddies usually encountered. The other caddies and golfers were trying to keep him quiet, saying, "Dude, you gotta lay off of her." To the amazement of the other caddies, Diane was able to handle it until they hit the seventeenth hole. Diane said, "We were on the seventeenth green just about to be done with the whole round. There was some kind of a cut in the grass all the way along, and he said something about a French lip. I don't even know exactly what it was he said, but it was just disgusting. I was done. The next hole had this water hazard that went straight down fifty feet. He made this comment and I just went to that thing, took his bag off my back, and threw it in the water—thousands of dollars worth of golf clubs! Then I just walked off the course. I remember hearing clapping. I don't know if it was the other caddies or if it was his golfers. Whatever it was, he had crossed the line and I was done. I was shaking. I went back to the caddyshack. He complained. I think he got reprimanded or something, but nothing serious. I was suspended for two weeks. But our caddy master knew about him. Our caddy master would tell me to still come to the course every day when I was suspended. He knew that they would run out of caddies. Caddies would wait for a couple of hours, and if they didn't get a loop they'd leave. He would pick up the phone and say, 'The only caddy here is one who's suspended.' They would say, 'Let her go up; I need a caddy.' So I still ended up caddying that entire time. It was one of those things where it was, 'I'm not taking this anymore.' I was legendary for that. Probably still."

Make it real—be uniquely and authentically you.

When people feel they can relate to you after you have shared your story with them, you've taken a big step in getting them on board with your risk taking. For them to be able to relate to you, they have to experience the real you, they must know it's authentic—not some varnished, glossy version of yourself that you're trotting out because it's what you think they want to hear from you. If someone is going to take a risk on you, or for you, or with you, they want to know exactly who they are dealing with. They want the truth. Your stories must communicate the following in order to portray your real, unique, and authentic self: your values; your summits and your cliffs, and your leading strengths and your challenge points; your personal brand.

Your values

You want your stories to illustrate that you are willing to take risks, but that when doing so you adhere to your value system. You want your stories to illustrate your value system. Your values are what you stand for. One of the most powerful bonds you can establish with others when taking a risk is shared values. They build stickiness for when times are tough.

Diane's golf-bag-in-the-water story and Kim's promotion story both do a great job of communicating some of their core values in the context of their risk taking. Jan communicates some of her core values when she tells her story about founding PayTech. She tells how she said to people, "I want to build more than a company with just a whole lot of bodies in it. What I want to build is a work-life balance for women to understand that they're worth so much more in this industry. Because payroll is so thankless, and there's really no opportunity to grow...I want us to hire women that can be empowered to use their skills to help companies." In addition, when she hired her first employees, she made a conscious choice about how they would handle work-life integration, telling people, "I don't want to babysit people. They're women in business. They should be able to handle their job. If they can't, then they're in the wrong position here. But I want them to be able to leave at two o'clock and be able to go see their child sing at the mall. If they choose to work that evening, fine, just get the job done." That's how Jan has built her company. She's got over one hundred employees of which 90 percent are women which proves that works, and she makes sure those values come across when she tells her story.

Connie spoke about her moral compass, not being willing to risk beyond her value boundaries. In Chapter 3 I shared a comment of hers, "I am not willing to risk integrity for performance or anything that will have a longer term deleterious impact on the organization, my team or my personal reputation." Bindu commented, "In terms of risk taking the value of integrity is something that I look for if I am taking a risk with somebody. I need to have those highest levels of integrity and huge levels of commitment—wanting to do that work and take that risk." Annette said, "You have to really explore why it is you're taking the risk and what's lying underneath it all. It usually boils down to in myself either there's something that's going with my values or going against my values that's driving towards my life purpose or going away from my life purpose."

Your summits and your cliffs, your leading strengths and your challenge points

Your summits and cliffs are key experiences and events and milestones in your career. They are ups and downs you have experienced in your career journey and your lessons learned from those experiences. Include in your high-point stories specific facts and data about results and impacts, and don't lose yourself in the "we." Claim your "I." On the other side of this, no one is perfect, and it's hard to trust and therefore risk with someone who pretends they are perfect. Too often people are fearful of sharing their "cliffs"—their down moments in their career journey. That's a mistake. Artfully told, your "cliff" moments can be some of your most powerful stories. Your leading-strengths and challenge-points stories are there to back up what you claim to be—they illustrate your characteristics and tendencies. Anybody can claim to excel at something, but do you have the leading-strengths stories to prove it? Stories centered on your challenge points illustrate your ability to learn and adapt—essential characteristics for successful risk takers.

Jan shared a cliff story about tough times at PayTech. "During the recession we were running out of cash and we went into debt—my husband and I with our home and everything else to keep paying people and to keep the business going." She told me how scary it was, but that there was never one moment in that whole nightmare that she ever thought PayTech would not make it. She said, "I did make changes—not fast enough—but I did make changes, and we survived." It would be easy to think that Jan and PayTech are just one big success story, but this short acknowledgement of scraping the bottom of the barrel for a while makes her risk taking and subsequent success more realistic and accessible to others. I would risk with Jan, because I know she knows how to survive tough times.

Diane had a beautiful cliff story from earlier in her career related to managing people, how she learned from that experience and became a better and more accountable leader as a result. As the company she was working at grew, she started to hire people and grow her marketing team. She was hiring and managing people for the first time, learning by doing. Then the company decided to roll the creative team underneath her as well. She told me what happened. "That was really where I learned the difference of managing different types of people. What I had hired in my marketing team was people like me—open to criticism, go ahead, just give it to me straight. You live and breathe that as a marketer. You never got something back that didn't have corrections all over it. So now I am managing creative people, and I am not adjusting my management style. As direct as I would be and critical of the marketing people, I was that way with the creative people. It got to a point where the entire creative team of five people walked out on me and quit the company. That was unbelievable. It was so hard. You go through all of the 'It's them, they're flakes.' But I got back to blaming myself." Diane learned the hard way that there are different ways of managing people, and that you need to change yourself to make things work for your team if they're the right fit for the company. Diane thought the President of the company was going to yank that responsibility from her. Instead the President told Diane, "You broke it, you fix it. You've got to hire that team. You've got to build it back up. You've got to manage it." Diane reflected on the power of that lesson, acknowledging it as one of the most jarring experiences and learning opportunities she has had in her entire career. "It was horrible at the time, absolutely horrible. It is one thing I would never want to be any different than that was. It made me so much better as a manager." I would risk with Diane, because I know she knows how to learn from mistakes.

In Chapter 6 we covered knowing what your leading strengths are and acknowledging your challenge points. We explored why both of these are important to help you prepare for and be more effective in your risk taking. They also provide fodder for powerful stories you can share when positioning yourself for taking calculated risks. As with summit stories, include specific facts and data about how your leading strengths impacted outcomes. As with cliff stories include your key learnings and how you were able to change and grow from experiences in your challenge-point stories.

Your personal brand

If the person listening to your story were to remember just a handful of things about you, what would they be? How do your values, summits and cliffs, leading strengths and challenge points combine to create a personal brand that makes it crystal clear why this risk is the right risk for you? How does your personal brand show that this career risk is a perfect fit and aligns with everything that you are and that you have the potential to be? Your accomplishments, how you work, your reputation, your global experiences, visual aspects of how you portray yourself, who you associate with, organizations in which you have membership, what you do for fun, and many other factors all contribute to your personal brand. Well, so do your stories, because it is your stories that bring all the layers of your personal brand to life. Every opportunity you have to tell a story is an opportunity to either build or diminish your personal brand and impact how you position yourself for career-related risks and opportunities.

I recently met a woman who was looking for a job. There were four of us that heard her story the same afternoon; only one of us had known her prior to that. She told us the circumstances surrounding her departure from her last company and what she was looking for in a new opportunity. Unfortunately, in her case, she told her story in a way that significantly diminished her personal brand. In offline conversations afterwards, myself and the two others who met her for the first time that afternoon concurred that we would not risk personally associating ourselves with her in terms of a direct recommendation. In the telling of her story, she had come across as very negative, had shared some information that raised questions in our minds about her integrity, and she was inconsistent in what she told one person versus another. She was not someone that any of us would be willing to take a risk on, or with, or for. Be very careful in how you tell your stories. They should be an asset to building your personal brand and positioning you well for the risks you want to be able to take, not a detractor.

Mukta warmed up quickly to the topic of having a personal brand. "It's really important to brand yourself in terms of who you are and what you bring to the table. I've been very fortunate that I've been able to understand that. A lot depends on how you portray your attitude towards things. It's not a fair world out there. You've got to have an attitude that says you understand, but you are not going to give up. It's a can-do attitude that really brings out who you are as a person. It covers how optimistic you are, how patient you are, how you work with people." Mukta likes to see women incorporating their tendency to relate to people differently, integrating the warm and nurturing aspects of their personalities into their personal brand.

In Chapter 3 I shared with you Debbie's comments about the value she places on establishing a personal brand. Debbie shared another story that illustrates how your personal brand speaks for you even when you are not around. She was about twenty years into her career and had spent time in the printing and publishing side of the telephone company business, never working in the actual core business. An Officer responsible for network operations on the core side of the business asked Debbie to interview for an opportunity in his organization, reporting directly to him. Since she didn't know the first thing about the network organization and had no experience with that side of the business, her first thought was that someone asked him to interview her as a courtesy. They set a time to meet. During the conversation he felt she wasn't viewing herself as a real contender for the position. He paused their conversation and said to her, "Let me just stop you and make sure you understand. This isn't me interviewing you. This is me telling you you've got the job, and you deciding if you want it." Unlike the situation where Debbie had been asked to take over sales, in this case she did ask the Officer, "Why me?"

He said to her, "What I'm looking for is someone who can take apart very complex problems and situations and understand them and build a solution, even when you don't know the business. There's some value in you not having deep, embedded knowledge and a predetermined idea about how we need to build this thing going forward. You're going to have a huge team of people—many of who do not work directly for you. You're going to be leading your peers across all parts of this business, and you have a reputation for being able to collaborate with your peers, for being respected, and for being able to bring people together in a way that gets to a common purpose and vision and solution that they can see and it becomes a north star that people constantly keep sight of." He told her that every time he described the kind of person he needed to others in the network organization, they said, "That's Debbie. You have to interview Debbie Storey." She commented that this was her lesson about brand, saying, "Even though he told me those things, I still wasn't very comfortable. It was a big risk, a big job I was stepping into with a high risk of failure. But I had the confidence to know that if I failed, no one would believe it was because I didn't try hard enough, or I didn't have skills; and it was important for me to know that I would have a lot of people surrounding me to help make sure I didn't fail."

Chapter 8: The Critical Skill of Envisioning

For the grand total of ten dollars I did a marvelous exercise with a group of women at a workshop. The equipment for the exercise all came from the Dollar Store—two glass jars and eight bags of marbles. Prior to the session I emailed all the participants twelve questions. When the participants arrived at the session they were each given a little bag with twelve marbles in it. Each marble represented an answer of "YES," and each marble could be used to answer one and only one distinct question. They were then instructed to either allocate the marbles amongst two different jars or put them aside based on how they had answered each question. The point of the exercise was to reveal if the group was more inclined towards technical skills or visioning skills. Sounds of "clink, clink, clatter, clink" were heard as they dropped marbles into the jars or set them aside. At the end of the exercise, the "Technical" jar had more marbles in it than the "Visioning" jar, and there were also a fair number of marbles left over that the participants had not placed in either jar—their answer being "NO" to some of the questions. It was an excellent visual to represent the challenges and the opportunities related to the discussion we were about to embark upon. Vision and envisioning is a critical leadership skill, an absolute must-have as you advance into leadership roles. It's also a skill set that is fundamental to successful risk taking. Technical skills and doing great work will only get you so far in your career and in your risk taking.

Research has shown envisioning is a must-have capability for enterprise leadership, regardless of gender. We hear repeatedly how the ability to craft, communicate, and engage people in a shared vision are key traits of successful leaders. Your proficiency with these skills contributes to your leader identity. In a *Harvard Business Review* paper by Herminia Ibarra and Otilia Obodaru titled, "Women and the

Vision Thing," they shared findings from their research study: "Women are judged to be less visionary than men in 360-degree feedback. It may be a matter of perception, but it stops women from getting to the top...Being visionary is a matter of exercising three skills well: sensing opportunities and threats in the environment, setting strategic direction, and inspiring constituents...Three explanations for women's low visioning scores: Some women don't buy into the value of being visionary; Some women lack the confidence to go out on a limb with an untested vision; Some women who develop a vision in collaboration with their teams don't get credit for having one."[1] They provide pointers on how to strengthen your visioning skills: appreciate the importance of visioning, leverage (or build) your network, learn the craft, let go of old roles, communicate constantly, and step up to the plate. They write that one of the biggest developmental hurdles aspiring leaders must clear is learning to sell their ideas—their vision of the future—to numerous stakeholders, and that presenting an inspiring story about the future is very different from excelling in technical skills such as completing a strategic analysis or crafting implementation plans. They comment that a whole generation of women owe their success in getting to senior levels to a strong command of the technical elements of their jobs and a dedicated focus on accomplishing quantifiable objectives. Their caveat: "But as they step into bigger leadership roles—or are assessed on their potential to do so—the rules of the game change, and a different set of skills come to the fore."[1]

In numerous discussions I have had with groups on this topic, there is always lively debate on the findings and insights in the article, as well as acknowledgement of how relevant and important this is in the context of women in leadership. The point I must stress to you here is that the skill of envisioning is also critical when it comes to being successful in your risk taking. Many of the aforementioned concepts still apply, and there are additional nuances. In order for others to get on board with you in your calculated risk taking and be willing to risk on you, for you, and with you, it is imperative that you develop the critical skill of envisioning. In this chapter we will cover four areas to help you do that.

Combine passion and execution.

Challenge expected norms.

Explain the "why."

Display intent and focus.

The better you are at envisioning—no matter the application—the stronger the support base you will be able to build around you as you make decisions, take calculated career risks, and turn them into opportunity for you, your team, and your organization.

Combine passion and execution.

To be successful in your risk taking you need to effectively combine the envisioning and technical components. You need to clearly demonstrate that you have both the passion to fuel your ideas and the specifics to drive the execution of your ideas—a clear grasp of the strategy and the operational components of managing your risk. Over the past eight years as I launched my companies and programs, people have consistently commented how impressed they are by the passion and clarity I have in my vision, and in my detailed plans that sit behind the vision and are the arms and legs of executing it. My ability to risk serially, to have people back me in my calculated risk taking, and to have success with my risk taking has been predicated on having that combination of passion and execution. You will benefit from developing that combination for yourself.

Cathy's opinion is that women have an advantage in this arena. "If women are supposed to be the emotional and passionate gender, then what could be a better use of emotion and passion than painting a picture of the future? It doesn't matter what you are creating...It's got to be a flawless future. It's not exactly what the future will look like. But you've got to ignite an energy in the audience that makes people want to stand up and run towards the future so that we at least get halfway there in some reasonable amount of time." She also commented that you have to balance out the doing with the visioning and the emotion. "There has to be something after the passionate speech. At some point we have to actually do something. There has to be next steps and follow-through and strategies and tactics. You have to be good at that too. It's almost worse to build up all this enthusiasm and then have no plans for how we are going to deliver on that. So now let's form a committee and do the strategy and have the meetings. Let's design the dashboards by which we need to measure ourselves, because we need to actually get something done."

Cathy feels that she herself probably spent too many years not being emotionally expressive and conforming to the environment around her. She shared a recent personal experience on this front that reinforced for her the importance of adding passion to her execution. Over a thousand people convened for their most recent leadership conference. On the last day someone asked Cathy a question: "What does leadership mean to you?" She stood up in front of the entire audience and responded 100 percent from the heart, saying exactly what she felt. She told me she had not spoken that way to a crowd of accountants— or anybody else, for that matter—before, and she described the reaction. "I figured I was well-enough established that it wouldn't cost me, no matter what people thought. I didn't expect much of a positive reaction. The reaction I got from that struck me that there is an incredible thirst for the emotion as long as it is grounded in real capabilities and ability to get things done. It is powerful and people are thirsty for it. Reactions like, 'Never heard it put that way,' or, 'That needed to be said.' That tells me that there is room for people to be expressive."

Jan told me she could never have convinced people to work with her when she started PayTech if she didn't have the vision, the ability to articulate it, and the business plan that sits behind it. She told me that applied to the employees she hired as much as it did to the bankers she worked with, and that you always have to be excited about your vision. Melanie spoke about contagious enthusiasm. "Everyone has a different style. You can be low key and enthusiastic. I am more gregarious and outgoing and enthusiastic. People feel it. Enthusiasm breeds more enthusiasm and success breeds success. When people look at you, they see passion. Now what you are doing is painting that vision that every single person is going to fall in love with. Let's roll with it."

Challenge expected norms.

If what you are doing is in line with general norms and expectations, it isn't a risk. On the other hand, when you do something that's bold, grand, beautiful, exciting, and a departure from the norm for yourself and others—that's a risk. When defining and articulating your vision you need to be willing to challenge expected norms. When you are envisioning, aspects of challenging expected norms include: owning your voice, being willing to speak up and having the confidence to put your viewpoint forward even if it goes against the tide, and being willing to drive risky decisions.

Kim is challenging expected norms as she pursues her vision of achieving a new level of partnership between big business and women- and minority-owned enterprises. First at Aon and then at Willis she set about defining and building a whole new business model to better integrate the efforts of big business and minority- and women-owned enterprises pursuing and executing on large contracts that require a percentage of their spend to be directed towards women- and minority-owned businesses. She jumped at the opportunity to talk about this. "People call it a vision if it moves it from its current state. If you just talk about, 'Oh, this is what we are going to do to improve where we are currently at,' people will say that's tactical. In order to be considered a visionary you need to be able to deconstruct what currently exists and put it back together in a different way or model something completely different. But you are challenging the established norms, and in order to be able to challenge the established norms, you have to accept the fact that you are not going to be affirmed. Because people fight when you are challenging established norms!"

Kim told me about an opportunity she worked on with a team. The team was making some false assumptions, and typical group think

began to set in. Kim knew that in order for the team to come to the
best solution, everyone would have to own their own thoughts and
have the courage to break away from the traditional modus operandi
of going with the group in order to be liked. Despite the unspoken
pressure to go along with the group, Kim decided to speak up.
Ultimately the group ended up incorporating some of what she said
into the strategy and changing it. But they didn't necessarily like her
or applaud her for speaking out. She told me how she felt about that.
"You always want to be accepted and affirmed by your teammates. It
is important to work well together and to be nice. But
understanding—and I still sometimes struggle with it—it may be that
what I am saying may not be applauded in the moment because I am
taking them off the norm…The reality is there is still an emotional
part of me that is, 'I'll do it in the moment because this is the right
thing to do.' But afterwards it still does take some adjusting to being
the counterpoint, challenging a traditional standard." Kim said she
has learned it is not an option to not say anything. It is your
responsibility. No-one else is going to take ownership if you are in a
leadership role. She said, "I think that's one of the benefits of getting
comfortable with risk, getting comfortable with your voice, getting
comfortable with your values, owning who you are and being
comfortable with your perspectives, and not trying to be one of the
guys—which is one of the most absurd things. They aren't trying to
be one of the girls. Why would you want to try to be one of the guys?
We see things differently, that's why we are valuable. So own it!"

Successful envisioning is also about making tough and risky
decisions as you bring the vision alive. Some of those decisions may
challenge expected norms. Janet spoke about the importance of being
willing to drive risky decisions. "It may be that when a risky decision
has to be taken, any kind of existing bias that may be gender oriented
might intimidate the women. Just knowing the bias is there might be
very intimidating, and I think that tends to be a little silencing. I can
feel it myself when that happens…Breaking out and saying whatever
you are going to say at that moment is less likely than people who
might have been more vocal in comparison to you…so you'd be less

likely to be the one driving a risky decision. You might wait, essentially, for someone else to drive it. Build a network and peers around you to help support you in your being vocal. Practice expressing your views and having confidence about them, politely. All of this helps create a pattern of being vocal. The more you do that, then the confidence you have is easier to assert...because of course in those various situations there might be a lot of confrontation in the decision-making forum. People might try to bully other people. There might be a lot of emotion around these big, risky decisions. This requires for anyone some confidence to put your viewpoint forward, even though it might not be the popular point of view, or it might be traumatizing to some interests in the room. That is different than implementing a risky decision, because it may be that the most difficult moment is just making the decision...The risk takers will be recognized as such by driving those decisions."

Explain the "why."

You are making a decision to take a calculated risk with the objective of moving closer to your vision. In your mind the rationale behind your vision and behind your decision to take the risk that gets you closer to your vision is perfectly clear. The rationale—the "why"—may not be so clear to others. Explaining the "why" is a big contributor to getting people on board with both the vision and how your risk taking fits in the context of that vision. It's also a great way for you to obtain feedback and identify any gaps in the solidity of the vision and in your game plan to get there.

Mukta has found communicating why she is taking or declining a risk has been extremely important in helping her to build her support system—both at work and at home. She also recommends explaining the process you have gone through to get to your decision. She commented that if people understand the "why" and your how, if they have confidence you have done all the due diligence necessary, then it increases the likelihood of their support if things go well and if things don't go well. Sue expressed that there are times when a team might not understand why you want to take a certain risk. But in having that open dialog with them on the "why," you obtain their respect and support, even if they have a different point of view.

Diane believes that explaining the "why" behind your vision helps you to build your case for how you are going to get there, catch if you have missed something in your plans, justify why you are ready for the next step in your journey, and validate if your vision and plans are accurate. Diane suggests validating the accuracy of your vision and your plans by looking at others who have traveled a similar road and seeing how they describe themselves in terms of what they have done, even to the point of looking at their LinkedIn profiles. Then look at what you've done to see if you can describe yourself in that same way, or if you still have gaps you need to address. Diane elaborated, "It's more than just, 'Hey, I want to be here.' I can't tell you how many times in managing people they would come to me and say, 'I want to be this, and I think I can be this.' My question would be, 'Why do you think that?' They don't have an answer. I know their answer is, 'Because I want it.' That's not a vision." Diane said that for her a vision is, "Here's what I want and here's what I've done that shows that I am ready for that," or, "Here's what I am doing that tells you that I am getting ready for it."

Katie tied explaining the "why" back to her penchant for storytelling. "In order to tell a good story you have to have good reasoning behind it. I don't think that the storytelling perspective can work if you can't thoroughly explain why you are suggesting that risk should be taken. If people don't believe your delivery, you're also going to struggle. So delivery and reasoning are really important. If you are comfortable enough in what you believe and you feel strongly enough about what you believe, you shouldn't feel uncomfortable trying to share that and trying to make other people see your thought process."

Display intent and focus.

Without intent and focus, opportunities will pass by you without you even realizing it. Successful execution of a vision and drawing people towards you as both you and they take a risk on that vision requires that you display disciplined intent and focus. In the absence of your intent and focus, potential supporters will align themselves with other individuals in whom they sense a greater degree of commitment and planning of how to achieve the vision. I asked interviewees to describe how they see intent and focus being characterized, if they are more willing to risk with someone that displays intent and focus, and how important intent and focus are in the envisioning component of risk taking. The resounding consensus was that intent and focus are a big deal.

Maureen responded, "Absolutely, no doubt about it. It's a leadership thing. The person that I am grooming to ultimately take my place, she is a risk taker. She prepared herself so well for her interview and completely put herself out there. She wrote an entire plan up, and in her second interview with me she said; 'This is what I would do.' There is not a week that goes by that she doesn't come into my office and say, 'Maureen, I have an idea.' Or, 'What if we...?' " Maureen elaborated that she sees intent and focus in people when "...they share their vision with me. They share their plan, their ideas, and their passion. You can feel it in them. They are passionate, they are driven, and they are goal oriented." She concluded by saying that what always brings it home for her in terms of buying into someone's vision and their risk taking is when they are able to tell her, "This is how I am going to get there." She said, "It's one thing to talk about an idea. It's another thing to actually have the nuts and the bolts and the plan on how you are going to get there."

Cathy jumped into this topic with equal vigor. "It absolutely influences others. When you feel that intent, and focused, and deliberate, and sure, most people are drawn to that. That is somebody you want to team with. It is purposeful. Most of us are drawn to that. When you are risk taking you need to dig. You are inherently unsure of yourself in some aspect of what you are doing. That's the whole idea of risk. You have to almost overcompensate being intentional and focused and deliberate. You need to force yourself to be sure. You need to do it intentionally, as it is not going to come as naturally as when you are in an arena where you don't feel any risk, or where it is easy to be focused and intentional, and not distracted by that uncertainty."

Cathy shared one of her own recent missed beats on this front. "I missed a beat last Monday. I could hear myself on every call I was on. I felt inarticulate, I felt tentative in my choice of words. I felt tentative in my gut. At the end of the day I felt exhausted and unimpressed with myself. I've no idea what anyone else's perception was, but I was wholly unimpressed with myself, and I did not want to relive that day…You can't have that uncertainty bleed over into your approach. You've got to step away, take a deep breath, so that when you step forward you do so with intent. You know it when you see it in other people. You are drawn to that. It's strong and sure, and not without some vulnerability. But you need to move with certainty, even if you later need a correction." She continued on, describing what she did to regroup her intent and focus. She literally and figuratively stepped away. The figurative part was stopping, reflecting, debriefing in her head, and laying out a whole new approach to how she was going to re-engage. The literal part was changing up her work environment for the next day to provide some fresh perspective. "I did not ever find a reason to leave my kitchen counter Tuesday. It was my base of operations. I stayed home; I was in isolation. I drove every call and written project from here so that I could not be distracted from putting my focus and attention where I needed it to be."

Chapter 8 Notes

1   Ibarra, Herminia, and Obodaru, Otilia. "Women and the Vision Thing."
    Harvard Business Review (January 2009, reprint): 1–9.

Chapter 9: Communication Is Key

Effective communication helps you build engagement and trust when taking risks in your career. It helps you test your ideas and make them better, and it helps to build confidence in your preparedness for and likelihood of success at taking and navigating career risk. Judgments about these factors are often made based on how we communicate with people and how they interpret what they hear from us. It's about what we say and how we say it, what people hear and how they hear it. Communication is key as you shift yourself on your risk-taking continuums. In this chapter we are going to cover what makes for effective communication in the context of your risk taking, and how you can invest in developing your communication skills for risk taking.

Debbie focused on engagement. "I think great communication drives high engagement. In my experience, to lead bold strategies and lead people to achieve bold visions, you have to communicate in a way that they can understand the strategy, connect themselves to that strategy, and understand the role they play in getting there. That's how I've been able to get every individual feeling like they're on board. Really good leaders motivate others to walk through walls to achieve the team's objectives."

Cathy focused on engagement and testing your ideas. "Communication is absolutely mission-critical because where there is risk there is uncertainty. If the right thing to do was clear and everybody agreed, there would be no risk...You better make sure people are with you before you move, because when you are taking risk and you turn and there is nobody alongside you, that is dangerous...You need the funding. You need the approval. Whatever it is, you need to get to the finish line. Whether it is the influencers, the outright supporter, the ultimate decision maker, the finance guys with the money, whatever it is. All of those stakeholders—you would be well served to make sure they are with you. The communication is fundamental…You can also test your own thinking. If you are forming hypotheses and ideas, the territory may not be very familiar to you. So it can also be very instructive, coming to the right path forward. Listen to other points of view. Feedback can be very active—talk and listen as much as possible before you calculate your risks, and then be decisive about it."

Vlada spoke about how trust builds from effective communication. "Perception is influenced by the way a person behaves, interacts, speaks, and the way that [s]he can get this connectivity to people. That is extremely important. I truly believe this is when things start working. It takes some time to build this trust and belief in you." It is highly unlikely that people will support you in your risk taking if they don't trust you, so it is necessary to understand how effective communication builds trust. In *The Jossey-Bass Reader on Educational Leadership,* by Margaret Grogan, two of the contributing authors— Andy Hargreaves and Dean Fink—write, "Trust is a resource. It creates and consolidates energy, commitment, and relationships. When trust is broken, people lessen their commitment and withdraw from relationships, and entropy abounds."[1] Hargreaves and Fink write that clear, high-quality, open, and frequent communication, sharing information, telling the truth, keeping confidences, and being willing to admit mistakes all underpin communication trust.[1]

Whichever way you look at it, your ability to communicate effectively is key to getting people to support you in your risk taking. Without effective communication you could lose the confidence, commitment, engagement, and trust of key stakeholders necessary to support you in your risk taking.

Effective communication in the context of risk taking in your career

Communications is a huge topic, so keep in mind that here we are zeroing in on what makes a difference to support you in your risk taking in your career. Here are ten starter tips. I encourage you to examine your own communication style and identify other factors that may need attention.

DO! Follow your instinct and just ask for it.

If you truly believe in the risk you wish to pursue, you have to be willing to pave the way forward by voicing your goals and aspirations to others and asking for what you need.

Annette Reid joined Aviva when she graduated from one of Edinburgh's universities. After a short period of time the trainees were required to select which track they wanted to go down—underwriting or claims or sales. Annette didn't want to go down any of those traditional tracks. Even though she had only been at the organization six months, she listened to her instinct and took the bold step of telling them what she really wanted. "I already had a gut feeling that being a technical insurance professional was not what I wanted to do. What I was getting the most energy out of in those first six months was people leadership. I hadn't been exposed to it myself, but I was watching other people who either ran the Operations Departments or spent a lot of time leading and developing their people. So I said to them, 'Would you consider setting up a fourth track, which is about Operations Management, which will help me focus specifically on large-scale people leadership?' It was worth asking the question, because they did. As it turns out, there was a girl in Manchester who was having a similar conversation. Two of us went down this brand new track that was created specifically for us. This shaped the career I then ended up in."

DO! Be clear and specific.

It's not enough to ask for what you need in broad terms. You need to be precise about what you require to move forward in your risk taking.

Maureen learned the lesson about the need to be clear in her brief sojourn away from Lettuce Entertain You. During the initial "courting" period between Maureen and the company that was looking to bring her on board, Maureen identified what was important to her. Three of those priorities were being able to run her own show, having the guarantee of Partner, and flexibility in her schedule. To her surprise, the constructs of their offer did not align with the priorities she had communicated to them. "When we sat down for the final negotiation—or the second-to final-negotiation—they presented me with this package which was not anywhere close to what we had talked about. I looked at this piece of paper they had put in front of me. I was aghast. I said, 'This is not at all what we talked about. I don't know that this is going to work for me.' I walked away.' " When they asked her to meet again in a couple of days, she agreed, using that time to prepare another communication that was very clear and specific about her expectations. "When I went back to meet with them I laid out— again—exactly what it was that my expectations were. That was the communications piece. This is what I want if I am going to make this change. As much as it didn't work out, I did communicate all along. You've got to communicate what you want if you are going to take a risk and leave or move within."

DO! Negotiate.

You might not get exactly what you initially asked for to support you in your risk taking. That doesn't mean you don't take the risk. Know what else would help you move forward, and negotiate for that.

Maureen told me what transpired when she returned to Lettuce Entertain You after her brief time away. She was now taking the calculated risk of pushing hard for Partnership at Lettuce. "As much as my background has been sales, I really didn't know that much about negotiation. I've been in a role where everybody wants what Lettuce does, so it was easy. But I never had to have a hard negotiation—a back and forth—and be willing to walk away from the table. I had that in this last situation. A friend of mine—male—who is a great negotiator gave me the things that I needed to weave in. He said, 'They are going to try and dominate the conversation in many regards, but you need to say things like, 'You know what, can I share a couple of things?' You need to interject yourself.' " Maureen told me she practiced the dance of "That's not quite the number that I was thinking of," followed by sitting back and being prepared to say, "This is what I was thinking of." Maureen made sure she was as prepared as she could be for negotiations.

DO! Provide decision-making frameworks and think analytically.

Use decision-making situations as an opportunity to step forward, lead, and position yourself as a savvy and rational risk taker.

Janet built on her earlier point about driving key decisions in order to be viewed as a risk taker. She spoke about the communication aspect of this. "A lot of times the person who leads the group out to a rational action is the one who is very poised and presenting a rational alternative. The ones who appear to be more ranting—whether they do it calmly or in an excited way—it's usually not very well taken at that point in the discussion...The conversations and the number of stakeholders that have to be in them tends to increase. Too many topics, too many stakeholders—it's very hard to come to a conclusion. So building a framework is a powerful thing. The person who can do it can also grab a leadership role at the discussion—a thought process that looks like what are we trying to achieve, what are the outcomes we are driving for, why do we think those are important, and what are the operational steps to get there. Organizing your thoughts so that people can see what it is they have to do. Someone who articulates that takes a lead role in driving the discussion."

DO! Develop alliances.

When formulating your communications strategy for your risk taking, identify what you can do on your own, and where you need to leverage other people as part of your communications strategy.

Kim highlighted the need for women to develop alliances in their career risk taking with people who are empowered because they have the ability to prenegotiate or the power to prebroach the subject on your behalf. She commented that many young professional women may not have enough oomph to challenge something all on their own—that they need to develop alliances with other men and women who have their back, who are in favor, and who have political backing. She stressed that being able to work those informal networks and knowing where formal and informal power lies is something that women have to be savvy about, that if you don't have that backing you are out on an island. Kim said, "It's easier to accept difficult information from someone that looks like yourself. So if you start talking about being visionary, if you start talking about challenging norms and expressing big bold ideas, if I'm in a room of all white males that don't have a relationship with me and that aren't connected with me, and somehow we haven't had some kind of bonding, they are going to see my statements—no matter how brilliant—as a threat, and it will get shot. It doesn't matter what it is. I don't know many times it takes for a concept to be introduced for people to say, 'OK, it's not so scary; I don't want to kill it.' I don't know if they do that in the Eastern cultures, but in Western [cultures] we are going to kill it if it looks wrong, unless it comes from someone who undeniably has power."

DO! Listen and actively seek feedback.

The vast majority of people around you want you to be successful in your risk taking. Their input and advice—solicited or not—is well intended. Listening to them and welcoming their feedback will help you tighten up your strategies and tactics and ultimately be more successful in your risk taking.

Debbie commented, "You have to be able to listen. Listening is a huge part of leadership." Recall Bindu's comment in Chapter 6: "Feedback helps you to get new ideas, test your own ideas, and keep your feet on the ground. The minute you stop getting or soliciting feedback, you are bound to make a mistake." That was in the context of knowing yourself, but it applies equally to testing your assumptions and plans as you prepare for your risk taking. Make sure you are engaging in active listening. Ask questions, dig deeper, make the most of the opportunity to identify what you might have missed, both in terms of preparing for the risk taking and in terms of the broader opportunity itself.

DO! Tailor your communications content and style to the audience.

The risk you are about to take touches many different stakeholders. You need them all on board to help you be successful. Don't adopt a one-size-fits-all communication strategy with your stakeholders. Tailor your content and style to the needs of each audience so you can effectively "sell" your risk to them.

Pam commented, "Knowing your audience and structuring your communications based on that audience is key. I always think of it in terms of a 'what's in it for me?' type of message. You can be the most influential if you are communicating to them why it's important for them and why it is important for the business, as opposed to what is important for you sitting there being the communicator. It's important for you to be connecting with the audience." Nancy Sharp said, "Know who you are selling to. If you are sitting across the table, selling to a white, sixty-year old-man, your dialog had better be different than if you are talking to your manager, who is thirty-four and a midlevel manager. Your dialog had better be different if you are talking to a woman versus talking to a man. It better be age specific, gender specific. You need to know a Boomer is going to listen to something differently than a Gen X. You need to know your audience. Have a pregame meeting to ask the best questions and listen with intent so that when you respond, you respond to what they are looking for."

DO! Practice your delivery.

You often only get one shot to make your case when taking a risk. Don't blow it. Practice, practice, practice what you are going to say and how you are going to say it.

Reflect back on Maureen's comments earlier about practicing for her Partnership negotiations. Melinda zeroed in on this topic. "I rehearse before communications. I always think ahead as to what can I say and how can I say it. That gives me the best chance of getting what I want. I am fairly calculated about it. I have had many people—particularly in HR—who have valued my coaching because they said that I can phrase things in a way that is so much more non-confrontational or easier than they would have thought of. But it didn't always come naturally. It came as a result of thinking hard about how I would get there."

DO! Get the recognition.

It's your risk. You're the one that has been brave enough to envision it, pursue it, secure the backing and support, and potentially lead and navigate others through it. Don't let all of that be attributed to others. It doesn't mean that you can't share in some of the recognition. But make sure you get the recognition that you rightfully deserve.

Nancy Mueller described an alternative strategy of using your network to secure recognition for your risk taking. "It's hard to go and try to grab recognition for yourself. Recognition comes when people know what has occurred. Generally your network is supporters, friends, people who want to see your success and you want to see theirs. Use your network for the recognition." She shared an example she had been privy to recently—a situation outside of her work setting. The individual who had started the initiative concerned was quite hurt they were not getting the recognition when the initiative had taken off way beyond anyone's dreams. Nancy shared how as a group they directed people to remember how they actually started the initiative, thereby calling to attention and recognizing the critical role that individual had played. "It was gratifying for the individual, and it made everyone else feel better that they hadn't left somebody out. So if you're the person not receiving the recognition, we all know how that feels, but if you're not recognizing someone because of oversight or because you don't know to do so, you actually feel bad yourself too. We felt much better ourselves, plus the person got the recognition that they really deserved. They felt bad that they weren't getting it but didn't know how to say anything, and didn't know for sure if this had all snowballed from something they had started."

DO! Silence the monsters outside your head and inside your head.

It's extremely hard when taking risks to not doubt yourself along the way, to not question who you are, and what gives you the right to think you can pull it off. Even serial risk takers fall prey to that at some point or another. If they say they don't, I would take the position that they are not being truthful with you or with themselves. It's a normal part of the process of risk taking. This negative pressure can come from real live naysayers and your internal naysayers. In everything I have risked on—even though I have had many supporters—I have had people who did not believe I would be successful, and I have had times when I have doubted my own ability to be successful. The trick is, while you might hear those voices pipe up outside and inside your head, just don't listen to them. Use your positive thinking, the successes you have already had, the support of family and friends and trusted colleagues who do believe in you to state your case for success and to quiet those external and internal monsters down. An additional strategy for those internal monsters in your head is to identify an alter ego for yourself or a visual artifact that you can call on to come out and slay them if they don't get themselves in line and pipe down. I have a penchant for the image of me wielding a lovely long sword as I navigate through my risk taking. I build a mental picture of me striking down those noisy internal monsters when they get too loud and boisterous.

If I had combined the negative opinions of outsiders with the niggling doubts that sometimes arose in myself, I would not have left South Africa to build a whole new life for myself in the United States, I would not have walked away from partnership at Deloitte, I would not have built up my successful consulting company, I would not have launched my second business focused on development and advancement of women in the workplace through cross-generational collaboration and risk taking, I would not have launched gen-xyb™ High Tea, I would not have written this book, and I most certainly would not be on a journey towards realizing my full potential and becoming everything I can possible be.

Invest in developing your communication skills for risk taking.

Effective communication skills do not come naturally to everyone, but they are an important skill set to develop and apply to support you in your calculated risk taking. I have not found much material relative to communication in the context of risk taking. However, there are lots of excellent resources on the broader subject of communication and on the topic of women and communication that you can apply to yourself as you take calculated risks in your career. Here are some of my favorites.

Women Don't Ask, by Linda Babcock and Sara Laschever, is a must-read on differences in how men and women negotiate, and what factors affect women asking for what they want. The book explores what women lose out on by not putting their best foot forward at the negotiation table, the missed opportunities to negotiate that go far beyond the typical compensation issues, societal factors originating in childhood that play a role in male versus female behavior during negotiations, factors that impact women's willingness to ask for what they want, the long-term price of setting low goals and safe targets, and recommendations on how to approach the process of negotiation in a manner that leverages women's advantageous characteristics.[2]

"Leading Through Negotiation: Harnessing the Power of Gender Gender Stereotypes," a *California Management Review* article by Laura J. Kray, talks about appreciating the ways in which the bargaining table may be experienced differently by women and men, and how acknowledging the gender factor in negotiations can influence performance during negotiations and the outcomes realized. The paper also provides three key strategies for leveling the playing field, including doing your homework, learning to love the game, and challenging beliefs and assumptions.[3]

How women fare when negotiating in ambiguous situations is the subject of "When Does Gender Matter in Negotiation," a piece by K.L.

McGinn, Dina W. Pradel, and Hannah Riley Bowles that appeared in the Harvard Business School periodical *Negotiation*. The authors focus on ambiguous situations where the parties have little insight as to the limits of the bargaining range and appropriate standards for agreement. They highlight that in highly ambiguous situations it's more likely that gender differences will influence negotiation behaviors and outcomes. They take a deeper look at highly competitive situations (men step up their performance in competitive situations where outcomes are determined by comparing relative performance, tending to fare better) and situations where someone is negotiating for others (women perform better when negotiating on behalf of others than they do when negotiating for themselves). They write about strategies to neutralize gender differences in negotiation, including anticipating gender-related triggers, doing your homework, creating transparency around compensation and benefits, and articulating performance expectations.[4]

"Breakthrough Bargaining" by Deborah M. Kolb and Judith Williams that appeared in *HBR OnPoint* covers specific strategies to use during negotiations, irrespective of gender. The strategies counter one party having unequal power relative to the other bargaining party. The authors cover three different types of strategies: power moves, process moves, and appreciative moves. In power moves they write about offering explicit incentives, putting a price on inaction, and enlisting support. In process moves they recommend seeding ideas early, reframing the process, and building consensus. For appreciative moves they look at helping others save face, keeping the dialog going, and soliciting new perspectives.[5]

In the broader field of communications I recently added a new paper to my list of favorites. Deborah Tannen's *Harvard Business Review* piece, "The Power of Talk: Who Gets Heard and Why," offers superb insights into the differences in the linguistic styles between men and women, and how this influences who gets heard, who gets credit, and what gets done. What I find particularly intriguing in this article is her focus on how language also negotiates relationships. She writes, "Through ways of speaking, we signal—and create—the relative status of speakers and their level of rapport." She then explores dynamics of "One Up, One Down," writing, "Men tend to be sensitive to the power dynamics of interaction, speaking in ways that position themselves as one up and resisting being put in a one-down position by others. Women tend to react more strongly to the rapport dynamic, speaking in ways that save face for others and buffering statements that could be seen as putting others in a one-down position." From there she goes into how this plays out, the consequences, and how to factor your understanding of these dynamics into your own communications.[6]

If you want to get some great tips on not downplaying your accomplishments, read the Kelley School of Business's *ScienceDirect* paper "Communication essentials for female executives to develop leadership presence: Getting beyond the barriers of understating accomplishment" by Anett D. Grant and Amanda Taylor. They cover changing the way women talk about accomplishments in order to improve leadership presence and aid in promotion. They dig into differences in how men and women talk about accomplishments, honing in on six communication essentials women should utilize to greater effect: starting strong, staying succinct, dimensionalizing content, owning voice, controlling movement, and projecting warmth.[7]

Many years ago I participated in a leadership development program for high-potential senior managers at Deloitte. The women running the program recently authored a *Harvard Business Review* article, "Women, Find Your Voice," by Kathryn Heath, Jill Flynn, and Mary Davis Holt, in which they look specifically at how performance in meetings matters more than you think, and the imperative for asserting yourself appropriately in meetings. They share what men see, what women feel, and what women can do to make themselves more effective in meetings, including mastering the pre-meeting, keeping an even keel, and making your language more muscular. They also briefly touch on what organizations can do to help ensure that women's voices get heard.[8]

Even though these materials are broader in their coverage of negotiation and various communication skills, as you read them you will see their relevance in the context of you leading yourself and others through your risk taking. Make sure to invest time and effort into building out your communication skills. Don't assume you have them, don't assume people you know have them, and don't assume that people you view as successful serial risk takers naturally have them. They come with work.

Chapter 9 Notes

1   Grogan, Margaret, with Hargreaves, Andy, and Fink, Dean (contributing authors). *The Jossey-Bass Reader on Educational Leadership.* Jossey-Bass, 2013: 462.

2   Babcock, Linda, and Laschever, Sara. *Women Don't Ask.* Bantam Dell, 2007.

3   Kray, Laura J. "Leading Through Negotiation: Harnessing the Power of Gender Stereotypes." *California Management Review* 50, no. 1 (Fall 2007): 159–173.

4   McGinn, K.L., Pradel, Dina W., and Bowles, Hannah Riley. "When Does Gender Matter in Negotiation?" Harvard Business School *Negotiation* 8, no. 11 (November 2005, reprint): 1–5.

5   Kolb, Deborah M., and Williams, Judith. "Breakthrough Bargaining." *HBR OnPoint* (February 2001): 87–97.

6   Tannen, Deborah. "The Power of Talk: Who Gets Heard and Why." *Harvard Business Review* (September–October 1995): 138–148.

7   Grant, Anett D., and Taylor, Amanda. "Communication essentials for female executives to develop leadership presence: Getting beyond the barriers of understating accomplishment." Kelley School of Business *ScienceDirect* (2013): 73–83.

8   Flynn, J., Heath, K., and Holt, M.D. "Women, Find Your Voice." *Harvard Business Review* (June 2014): 118–21.

Chapter 10: Your Role Diversification Strategy

Diversification is a good risk-mitigation strategy when making financial investments. It is also a good strategy to prepare yourself for greater success with risk taking in your career. Diversify yourself by expanding the breadth of what you do during your career. This can take the form of the type of roles you take on, the industries you work in, and where you work geographically.

In the *Harvard Business Review* article, "21st Century Talent Spotting," that I mentioned in Chapter 5, Claudio Fernández-Aráoz reports on asking 823 international executives to reflect on their careers and share what they felt had helped them unleash their potential. "Stretch assignments" was the most popular response (coming in from 71 percent of the respondents). Tying for second place—each mentioned by 49 percent of the respondents—were job rotations and personal mentors.[1] Someone that is willing to raise their hand for a stretch assignment is a risk taker. The person who is willing to embrace the challenge of the unknown and the learning that comes with job rotations is a risk taker. Risk takers rise to the top. That person can be and should be you. Francene wisely advised, "Be willing to say yes even if you are terrified that you will not be successful...Sometimes that's the difference between men and women. Men are more apt to say yes and figure it out later. Women sometimes more have self-doubt." Connie advises, "Avoid being wedded to a specific title. C-suite titles are lovely things, but what is the group of skills that you might have that will allow you to adapt? For most women—in terms of risk and being able to manage risk—that means that we must be willing to take new jobs and different kinds of roles." Tony said, "Risk taking for me is a differentiator. When I look at leaders in organizations and those individuals that are working for me, those that are taking risks are challenging the environment and are helping us think differently."

Irrespective of the type of role-diversification opportunity you are in front of, you need to be willing to go for it. In this chapter we are going to cover the case for role diversification, types of role diversification, and going global. In Chapter 11 we'll get into how to prepare for a new role.

The case for role diversification

Differentiating yourself, not playing it safe, being comfortable and confident in your ability to prove yourself again, willingness to try new things and your ability to be successful with them, aligning with your personal interests, displaying ability to renew your capabilities and how you value time to learn, bringing fresh perspective—these considerations are just some of the factors that speak to your abilities and effectiveness as a risk taker. They come from being willing to take on different roles. Janet commented that, "People who have fear or don't have a thick skin try to hue very close to what they are good at doing. But the act of renewing your capabilities is so important for most jobs to make real progress at the executive level. Someone who is in a process of occasional dramatic renewal is much more likely to look more capable at a senior level than someone who hasn't during their career. [You] acquire a certain level of risk tolerance."

At the request of the CEO, Nancy Mueller stepped out of the Chief Actuary role at Zurich North America and took on the Chief Operating Officer role. It's not a normal path for an actuary to become a COO, and she didn't know much about operations. On the other hand she couldn't imagine doing the same thing for the rest of her career, and she didn't want to get bored and wonder what it could have been like if she had tried something different. She made the move and since then has successively gotten additional responsibilities. Nancy said, "Once you've changed roles, you have a perspective that it isn't quite as scary the second time…That's the second time I truly had to think about what's the right thing to do because it's safer to stay in the job that I'm trained for. I think I had a reputation here in the company. There was a period of time where I had to prove myself again. You don't really think of having to do that over and over again, but it's also a good learning. Now there are people that don't know I have an actuarial background. Many folks have a functional profession—whatever you went to school for, you have that to rely on. But then gain enough confidence and look at yourself and say, 'Where are my interests?' Seek out opportunities that aren't perhaps as strictly within your formal training...Be willing to go and look beyond the day to day." Karen pointed out that, like Nancy Mueller, all the women on the Executive Leadership team at Zurich North America have a story to tell about taking risks with role diversification, be it through lateral moves that may have been perceived as not directly upward, or not taking the traditional career path, or taking a lead in a special project, or taking a role outside of one's traditional discipline. She said, "I think of Kathleen Savio in particular. She came in on the Communications side and is now President of Programs and Direct markets. She doesn't have an underwriting background. She doesn't have that traditional experience. But what she does have is breadth of experience. She was able to get experience across different areas of the company, and that has coalesced into running one of the key businesses that's driving a lot of the growth for this year."

Erin said, "Unfortunately it's not a ladder in the world of success. In the world of the professional environment, it's a scatter plot." In a subsequent discussion she elaborated. " 'It's a scatter plot' means being willing to try new things...You have to be willing to step outside of your comfort zone, and if your job description says that you're responsible for doing x, y, and z, you have to be willing to try a, b, and c. You have to be willing to do that so that others see that your potential is immense and you may have started in one place but you could end up in a completely different place. In the meantime you could find something that you didn't know you would like or that you didn't know you had an interest in." Leslie built on the scatter plot concept. "Young people do look for a specific path—I do this, then I do this, then I do that. People with more experience behind them start to say, 'But I want to do what I want to do', or, 'I want to do what interests me.' I think the scatter plot gets to be broader and perhaps even more utilized by more experienced people than the younger people."

Risk takers that are willing to take on new roles bring fresh perspective. Debbie spoke about the value this provides. "One of the greatest dangers is when a successful business is thinking you can keep doing the same thing—just more of it, and faster—and that will lead to continued success. We live at a time of such incredibly rapid technological and competitive change—and what got you here is not going to keep you here in almost any industry today. We as business leaders—everyone—have to be willing to take off the blinders and seek new, diverse and different ideas, and be willing to explore and try different things and different paths forward. Women need to understand that not having deep embedded knowledge is an asset in a time of deep transformational change. When you have built the thing you are leading, it can be very difficult to unbuild it and be willing to change it and take it apart...That's one of the things that women have a great opportunity to do. Women need to say yes to opportunities, even when they don't have the precise experience to step into that new role."

Types of role diversification

When you vary what you do and where you do it, you are diversifying yourself and preparing yourself to be a more effective risk taker, and you are sending messages to others about your risk-taking propensity and success with taking risks. Let's look at what different types of role diversification you can avail yourself of, and what they say about your effectiveness at risk taking.

The role for which I have no prior experience

This role tells people you are an effective risk taker by communicating: *I can adapt quickly into new circumstances.* What else do you think it says about you?

When Jan worked for a company called Integrated Payment Products (part of American Express), she was asked to take over payroll even though she hadn't done it before. Bindu got an opportunity within Aon-Hewitt to take on a service delivery role for the Asia-Pacific market for the Payroll Outsourcing business which she had no prior experience with. Annette was asked to be a Personal Lines team leader over a team of twenty people at Aviva with just a year of underwriting and operations experience under her belt. Going into it she had no leadership experience. Annette said, "They took a risk on me and I willingly accepted the risk. To this day it was probably the most developmental experience I've ever had. I suddenly found myself with brokers looking at me, saying, 'What's the decision, what's the rate, what's the cover?' I had customers phoning me and saying, 'Where's my policy, my endorsement, my green card—if it was a travel policy?' I had the team of twenty looking at me, saying, 'What's the decision on this? Can I override that?' Suddenly I had to just step up and be this leader, be this decision maker. It was an amazing experience, and I learned so much by taking that risk, jumping in at the deep end and trusting myself that I could do it but also that there would be support if I needed it." Much of Debbie's career has involved stepping into roles or new parts of the organization that she knew nothing about. In a twenty-year career at Northern Trust, Connie has held ten roles in the company. Her insights: "I think sometimes as women—and certainly research has shown—we think we have to know everything. I am not saying all women, but we think we have to know everything before we move into a new role, we have to check all the boxes and we know that is not realistic or even what is considered."

The blank-page role that has never existed before in this organization

This role tells people you are an effective risk taker by communicating: *I'm not afraid of ambiguity. I bring structure and order to the undefined.* What else do you think it says about you?

Leslie thrives on taking on roles that have never existed before in the organization. Two of her biggest roles—including her current one—started with a blank sheet of paper in terms of a job description.

She spoke about this type of experience. "The positive is you get to have an impact on what the role looks like. The negative is there's no precedent, no one to talk to, no track to run on. It's just every day you are trying to figure it out on your own. So it can be a little bit lonely and scary at times…It's that experience that I use when some days I am not sure exactly what I am supposed to be doing or how I am supposed to be doing it, because there is no roadmap. One of the reasons why I am well suited for these kinds of positions is I think I am better suited for creating things or fixing things than I am at maintaining them." Leslie observed that from her personal experience there are probably more women that don't want to take the risk and wing it when there's a blank-sheet-of paper-role because they first want to know how they're going to feel good about making progress before diving in. Unfortunately those answers aren't always clear upfront. Her counsel on how to combat that—you need to ask questions such as: how will I be measured, what does success look like, how will I know I am accomplishing what it is I am setting out to do? There is another aspect of a blank-page role that often stops women from taking the risk—what if it doesn't work out? Leslie commented on this. "If it is truly a role in which it's a blank sheet of paper, there's a certain amount of confidence you have to have that if it doesn't go well for some reason that something else will be available to you. Some people will want to ask that question, 'What if this doesn't work out, then what?' In the roles I've taken, I've never asked the question, 'Then what?' I've just had this personal sense that if something doesn't work out I'm still a valuable employee of the organization, and we'll figure something out."

The role that is a lateral move or a reverse move

This role tells people you are an effective risk taker by communicating: *I prioritize growth and outcomes over titles. I am dedicated to the continued pursuit of my personal passion and career vision, whatever the path that takes me there.* What else do you think it says about you?

After being at TIAA-CREF for eleven years, Leslie took a three-year career break to focus on the development needs of her youngest son. Once he was able to get back into school on a full-time basis, Leslie knew she needed to get back to work. She interviewed at a number of places, including Gallagher. They made a strong case for her to join their Health and Welfare business. Even though she was set on the Pension industry and she felt the job was a step backwards in terms of level and income, she was intrigued by what her interviewers consistently told her. One said, "I guarantee you this organization is growing so fast the job you take today is not the one you will have three years from now." The other one said, "The job you have is not the one you will have. Come join the organization." They were right. She came on as an Account Manager, held a couple of roles within the local office, then had a Regional role, and now is in a Divisional International role.

For Francene it's about staying true to what her vision is for her life and her career. She's always viewed it as her responsibility to identify the experiences and development opportunities she needs to have, to do them, and to be willing to celebrate the learning in both successful circumstances and if it doesn't work out OK. She said, "People didn't get to define who I was. That was my job. You really need to answer these questions for yourself: what are you passionate about, what is it that you want to achieve, and what are you willing to invest to achieve your dreams? You need to get comfortable with yourself and say I am either willing to make the sacrifice or I am not. What I have seen other people do is [being] willing to take lateral moves."

The role that is a line position (as opposed to a staff position)

This role tells people you are an effective risk taker by communicating: *I'm in the feeder pipe for the top jobs in the organization.* What else do you think it says about you?

In "Spotlight On Thriving At The Top," authors Peter Cappelli, Monika Hamori, and Rocio Bonet, shared research in the *Harvard Business Review* in which they examined the biographies of leaders in the top ten roles at each Fortune 100 company and looked at trends since 1980. They compared 2011 data against the data from the first time they completed this study a decade ago, in which they used 2001 data. One of the diversity trends they looked at was the rate at which women secured their executive positions relative to men. "Women in the 2011 group had secured their executive positions about three years earlier in their careers than men—but very few of them had risen to the top, as was true for the 2001 group. Only 5 percent had made it to the highest level positions, compared with 17 percent of the men."[2] They shared an average time span of twenty-eight years for women compared to twenty-nine years for men to get to top-tier positions; and twenty-three years for women compared to twenty-six years for men to get to middle-tier positions. Women had been promoted sooner in each previous job than men in both the 2001 data group and the 2011 data group.[2] The authors commented on why they think women ascended faster and the ramifications. "We think the women ascended faster because they were riding a different elevator. Middle-tier female executives, for example, had held primarily function-specific roles, such as chief legal officer, general counsel, or SVP of human resources. Their male colleagues had held more of the general management positions that typically feed the very top executive jobs."[2]

The importance of roles in line positions was also mentioned in a 2012 McKinsey & Company paper by Joanna Barsh and Lareina Yee titled, "Unlocking the full potential of women at work." In a study of sixty corporations—almost all in the Fortune 500 or of similar size—only one-third of the companies participating in the study had at least 55 percent of their women vice presidents and senior vice presidents in line positions. Women basically exit out of the line roles pipeline fairly early. They write, "Women shifting into staff roles as they advance is not an issue in and of itself. But last year, we saw that two-thirds of women on Fortune 200 executive committees were in staff roles, and they have far lower odds of advancing to CEO than those in line roles...Early in the pipeline, women and men are distributed across line and staff roles at similar levels, but women begin a steady shift into staff roles by the time they reach the director level. Structurally, women do not have the same opportunities to benefit from sponsor discussions, and so they lack support to stay in the line. Line jobs are less flexible than staff jobs, so as women form families, staff jobs look more appealing; well-intentioned leaders often do not even ask mothers to consider a tough assignment. And women know that line jobs carry greater pressure."[3]

The role that is leading a transformational change initiative or a special assignment

This role tells people you are an effective risk taker by communicating: *I can operate outside of the traditional career hierarchy, I am not worried about what comes next, and I am really good at being a leading agent for change.* What else do you think it says about you?

Recall Debbie's comments about the great opportunities women have to take on roles leading transformational change assignments. That is exactly what Jennifer is doing in her Zurich North America Headquarters Business Lead role. Jennifer told me about it. "Zurich has created a Business Lead [role] who represents the business in all facets of a large scale transformational change. We want to make sure we're keeping the business objectives in mind, we're hitting our goals, and we're really representing what we want as employees and leadership." Jennifer got the call from Nancy Mueller on a Friday afternoon. Zurich's building lease was up, and they were looking at options for a location change. Executive leadership felt it was critical to have a leader in place to represent the business in the entire process and drive key decisions. They believed Jennifer was the right person to fill that role. It did not matter that she had neither real estate background nor Business Lead role experience. Jennifer took a week to mull it over and speak to people she trusted. She quickly realized it was something she couldn't pass up. She didn't know where it would lead or precisely what she was getting into, but she did know there were so many possibilities with it. She also knew it was a risk, especially in terms of what would happen after the three-year assignment was up. When colleagues expressed that concern to her, she told them, "Three years is really far away. The whole organization could look different by then, so I'm not going to worry about that, because life is a journey and this is exciting." Knowing that she had been successful in other roles, she accepted and jumped right in.

Ely, Ibarra, and Kolb discuss women leading transformational change in their article, "Taking Gender Into Account: Theory and Design for Women's Leadership Development Programs" (*Academy of Management and Learning Education,* 2011, Vol. 10, No. 3, pages 483-484), commenting that since women are often selected to lead in turnaround high-risk situations it's critical to develop the ability to assume a lead change agent role. This requires "improving their capacity to create a sense of urgency for change, craft and communicate a vision of the future, get stakeholder buy-in, and motivate and inspire people."[4] These skills should ring a bell in terms of key skills for risk takers discussed in prior chapters.

The role in sales or leading client relationships

This role tells people you are an effective risk taker by communicating: *I can be on the front line with our customers—the lifeblood of our business. I am responsive, I can think on my feet, be an effective advocate, and build bridges between stakeholder groups internal and external to our business.* What else do you think it says about you?

Married right out of college, Melanie and her husband headed to Evansville, Indiana. She went to work for Sears Roebuck. When Melanie told them she would like to be in their management-training program, they obliged. They put her in management training in the wig department. With a laugh she told me the response that played out in her head. "Oh my gosh how do I tell my parents? They took loans out to put me through school and now their daughter's in the Sears wig department." Melanie viewed the opportunity as a gift and took a risk. "I could have walked away from that and said, 'You know what, I don't want to be in the wig department. I want to be in fashion.' That's what my goal was. But I went ahead and did it. I took a risk. I said, 'I'm going to show them I can do a fabulous job and then I'll be able to move on. I'll move to a different department.' So the gift is I learned I could sell. I'd never sold anything before that. I didn't sell one wig to a woman. I sold two and three and all the forms and shampoos and pins and brushes. I became the number one wig sales person in all of Sears. When I interviewed at IBM I told them I was number one in wig sales at Sears and all the managers laughed. But I told them, 'This is a big deal because I learned I could sell.' " IBM hired Melanie. Like Melanie, Erin started her career right out of the gate in a sales role. Inspired by her entrepreneur grandfathers, Erin knew she wanted to be in a sales organization. After interning with Gallagher for two summers she joined them full-time in 2001. She started by shadowing someone in a sales position. Two and a half years later she was promoted and was able to have more interaction with prospective clients as she looked for new business. In July 2013 she was promoted to Area Vice President, selling completely on her own.

The skills that Melanie, Erin and others who have been in sales roles and/or leading client relationships have developed are the same skills that make them more effective at risk taking and hence good leaders. So what are those skills? One is balancing advancing the agendas of multiple stakeholders. Tony heads Citi Retail Services's largest client relationship. He said, "It's working that interesting and delicate balance between the organization and the client and trying to advance the agenda of both. Having those sales client relationship roles certainly gets you in a place where you have to make decisions. Not only do you have to take risks, but they have to be on the spot at times. Some risks will go well while others will not. There is always a ton to be learned. The feedback is immediate—you know where you stand after each interaction."

Other skills you need to be effective at for your risk taking and that you can learn from sales and client relationship roles are the ability to persuade and influence others, and the ability to handle increasingly complex responsibilities and scope of work. At University of Illinois Business Innovation Services Francene is responsible for leading the ongoing relationship with a client once the sale has been closed. She stressed managing the progression so that you can get to a point where you can say, "I have developed the skill set. I have developed the track record of being successful with a small and medium size client and I am asking for the opportunity to handle the larger deals." In Francene's opinion it's not asking for a favor; rather it is saying with your skills and ability and track record here is why you are the best person to do this.

Listening, learning, and the ability to develop trust are necessary skills for risk taking in your career. People won't risk with you if they don't trust you, and they won't trust you if you aren't a sharp listener and learner. When Pam was at ADP she led relationships with clients who had anywhere up to seventy thousand employees—high profile clients with big market names. In her opinion the best place to learn these skills is by being in a client relationship management role. "Anyone looking to be at a senior level at a company needs to spend time with their customers. You can read all the reports you want and have metrics on client satisfaction and all of that. It is not the same as meeting your clients." Nancy Sharp was one of many that commented on how great women are in client relationship management roles. "I think women are natural born relationship managers. Everything they do in their life they are building relationships. They build them much differently than men. They are much more communicative. They listen. They tend to build better teams. They want collaboration."

The role of being an entrepreneur

This role tells people you are an effective risk taker by communicating: *I can take this outside. I can build something from nothing. I have a vision and I will bring it to life. I am a survivor.* What else do you think it says about you?

Jan incorporated PayTech in 1999. Their first large client was Graphic Packaging, a division of Coors. Today they have over one hundred employees across twenty-six states and they continue to hire aggressively. Yanyan's SN Mandarin language school is now one of the top three language schools in Shanghai with thousands of students coming through their doors every year from over one hundred twenty countries. Founded in 1983, Nancy Sharp's company Food For Thought Catering enjoys an esteemed place amongst Chicago's special event planners. They are on the preferred caterer lists for distinguished venues such as The Adler Planetarium, 19 East Event Gallery and The Field Museum. They also have a contract foodservice portfolio with clients such as the School of Art Institute of Chicago, Sidley Austin LLP and BP. Melanie's short-term accommodations company became part of a successful IPO. Melinda now has her own consulting company where she focuses on mergers and acquisitions. Bindu and her husband started a computer training institute when she was twenty-three years old. They all spoke about some of their key takeaways in their entrepreneurial roles: being willing to put yourself out there, believing in your ideas and not letting naysayers dissuade you, and being able to tough it out through bad times—all critical aspects of risk taking in any capacity.

Going global

Any of the afore-mentioned roles can have another diversification dimension added—the opportunity to go global. With the International Monetary Fund and other groups predicting that about 70 percent of the world's growth between now and 2016 will come from emerging markets, it's tough to imagine any professional career and the risks you engage in along the way not being affected by globalization in some fashion. So this is something you want to pay attention to and avail yourself of at some point in your career. Personal constraints may complicate the extent to which you can go global and for how long, but do what you can, and whenever possible learn a foreign language. Your ability to be more effective in your risk taking throughout your career is positively impacted by exposure to global experiences, insights into cultural context, and comfort with navigating across language barriers. Jon captured the broader imperative for global experience and developing your "cultural IQ" as part of preparing for risk taking. "We're in a global economy. We have sources of supply or markets or both internationally. The people that are going to reach the highest levels should have international experience. They should have this "cultural IQ" thing going for them. The earlier in your career you can establish yourself as an international person, that really sets the stage to get on that list of people who might be good for those pan-hemisphere jobs." Connie summed it up nicely, saying, "The reality is if you want to move up in an organization, relocation is a high probability. That is just a fact. For high potential individuals, relocating and having a global assignment is critical to getting your ticket punched."

Janet and Karen are Americans who both spent time living and working in Russia—Janet for three years in the early nineties and Karen for six months in the late nineties. They spoke about how their international experience made them less fearful of the unknown, increased their resilience, and opened their minds to taking into account different approaches and agendas when trying to engage others. Sue and Annette both moved from the United Kingdom to the United States with the respective companies they were working for in the United Kingdom. Sue spoke about working through the personal side of the risk all the way down to making a whole new circle of friends, the business side of the risk such as learning new legal constructs, and above all that willingness to put yourself into uncomfortable positions at times. Annette touched on the risks and consequences that the move entailed for her family and how it has ultimately benefited all of them and opened her up to taking bigger risks going forward. Mukta hails from India. She's had an international career with BP—first in the United Kingdom and currently in the United States. Mukta pointed out that all stages of your life are not equal when it comes to risking internationally. Now that she has children she has to factor in new considerations as she calculates the risk and opportunity associated with a possible move back to the United Kingdom. She commented that it's made her more cognizant of the theoretical and emotional sides of taking risk.

Vlada, Yanyan, and Bindu all pointed out differences in cultural expectations for women in countries such as Russia, China, and India. They discussed how pressure for women to focus on their families has significant impact on willingness of women in those cultures to take career risks and the extent to which they are supported when they do take those risks. Vlada moved from Russia to the United Kingdom to be the Executive Assistant to the global leader of BP's Lubricants business and then subsequently back to Russia to take on a sales leadership role within BP. Vlada placed emphasis on the difference in cultural expectations of women in Russia versus in the United Kingdom. She had to factor that into how she navigated the day-today realities of the international experience and into her decision to return home. Yanyan commented that whereas in many western countries women in their thirties and forties may just be getting into the prime of their risk-taking era, in China women feel that by that age their lifetime is behind them and risk taking would not be a real consideration. Bindu voiced that in India the mindset that still prevails is that while women do have careers, those careers are viewed simply as an opportunity for supplemental income for the family. They are not viewed as a serious pursuit in which risk taking should be applauded and pursued.

If all else fails obtain some limited degree of global exposure by finding opportunities to work with people in other parts of the world. Leslie works with team members in the United Kingdom. Toni worked with clients as far afield as Japan. Nancy Mueller reports into someone at the global headquarters in Switzerland. They shared how this has still enabled them to gain perspectives they would not have had otherwise, to figure out how to work well with others that might be on a different cadence than them, to get resolution to issues in times of conflict when what they take for granted in their environment is not the same elsewhere, and ultimately to thrive.

Having grown up in South Africa, spent a year in Israel when I was eighteen, moved to the States when I was twenty-six, and worked with colleagues and clients in different parts of the world I can personally vouch for the fact that going global increases your risk-taking preparedness. The imperative for finding some way to go global during your career journey is a critical part of your diversification strategy.

Chapter 10 Notes

1   Fernández-Aráoz, Claudio. "21st Century Talent Spotting." *Harvard Business Review* (June) 2014: 56.

2   Cappelli, Peter, Monika Hamori, and Rocio Bonet. "Spotlight On Thriving At The Top." *Harvard Business Review* (March 2014): 78.

3   Barsh, Joanna, and Yee, Lareina. "Unlocking the full potential of women at work." *McKinsey & Company* (April 2012): 6.

4   Ely, Robin J., Herminia Ibarra, and Deborah Kolb. "Taking Gender Into Account: Theory and Design for Women's Leadership Development Programs." *Academy of Management and Learning Education* 10, no. 3 (2011): 483–84

Chapter 11: Preparing for Your New Role

It's risky to move into a totally different role and transitions can be hard. The good news is that preparation can help you lay a great foundation for both the move and the settling in period. People will watch you closely to see how you do. The success of your transition speaks volumes about your ability to handle the risks associated with the role change and navigate through risk in general. One of my highly recommended books on the subject of job transitions is *The First 90 Days* by Michael Watkins, which provides a framework for leadership transitions and also covers some of the key challenges and situations you may find yourself in during the transition period. Another good book is *Right From the Start: Taking Charge in a New Leadership Role*, by Watkins and Dan Ciampa.

Robin J. Ely, Herminia Ibarra, and Deborah Kolb, in "Taking Gender Into Account: Theory and Design for Women's Leadership Development Programs," write that while both men and women encounter a myriad of challenges in career transitions, second-generation gender biases can make these career transitions more challenging for women. The *Academy of Management and Learning Education* piece discusses women being concerned about having to perhaps utilize a more masculine leadership style—which we know comes with its own repercussions—how to accommodate work-family demands, and stepping outside a comfort zone. They also write about women worrying about the ability to maintain a success trajectory the higher up they move in an organization, especially when a woman feels more vulnerable to the possibility of failure if there are few women represented in the organization's topmost ranks.[1]

Just like we did in Chapter 9 with communications, there is a risk-taking lens to apply to your transition efforts. Your ability to prepare for your transition effectively impacts your confidence and competence during the transition, the degree to which people will support you in your risk taking, and how you and others view your likelihood of success as you take the calculated risk of a role change in your career journey. In this chapter we're going to review five key components to your preparations.

Know when it's time to move.

Sometimes you will recognize this for yourself. Sometimes those that are close to you will see it first, and you may need the nudge from them. Peg, Francene and Maureen had career transitions that fell into the latter category. Remember Peg's story about the exchange with a Partner in her firm that made her realize she wasn't valued there? Francene had an instance where one of her mentors challenged her to move on. In Maureen's case it was a combination of input from a mentor and from a good friend who owned her own business, and the inspiration she got from a 2011 book by Mika Brzezinski, *Knowing Your Value: Women, Money and Getting What You're Worth*, published by Weinstein Books.

Keep your radar on and keep scanning the environment. Listen for cues and for opportunities—listening doesn't mean you have to make a change but to at least be open to opportunities and make a conscious choice whether to stay or move on. See what others around you are doing. Don't get too comfortable or complacent. The sooner you recognize it's time to move, the more time you are giving yourself to prepare and be calculated in your risk taking. That's way better than being surprised and having an unplanned and unexpected change foisted on you, which is a much harder risk to navigate through.

What got you here won't get you there.

If you haven't already had this conversation with yourself and with others, you should. To be successful with your calculated risk taking of moving into a different role, you need different resources and skills than what have helped you be successful in the role you are currently in. Maureen told me when she initially tried to make Partner at Lettuce Entertain You, she lacked resources that would advocate for her. "I've always been someone that has kept my head down, worked hard, come up with new ideas, continued to be strategic, always really giving it everything I had. I thought that at some point that would really be recognized. For me the wake-up call was when I was at an event and one of the younger Partners at Lettuce said to me, 'Maureen, you don't have a voice. You don't have a voice at the big table. You should be a Partner, but you don't have anybody at the organization advocating for you at that level.' That was a wake-up call for me. That started things rolling a in a completely different direction." We'll talk more about your advocates in a future chapter, but you need to recognize that those advocates are crucial as you prepare to risk into a new and different role.

In Chapter 8 we discussed how technical skills will only get you so far, how as you move into more leadership roles, different skills such as envisioning are necessary. You have to identify what else is necessary for you to prepare for your new role. Examine profiles of other people in the type of role you are transitioning to and see how they describe themselves in terms of their skills. If you identify something you don't have or that others consistently believe you don't have, then take the time and money to invest in some form of developmental experience to acquire it.

In the 2003 *Kravis Leadership Institute Leadership Review* piece "Gender Differences in Beliefs about Leadership Capabilities: Exploring the Glass Ceiling Phenomenon with Self-Efficacy Theory," Michael J. McCormick, Jesús Tanguma, and Anita Sohn López-Forment write about understanding and focusing on self-efficacy—confidence in one's capabilities—and how research has shown there is a gender difference in beliefs about personal capabilities. In one of the hypotheses, they state, "Women report having had fewer challenging leadership role experiences, less leadership training and development, and fewer mentoring experiences than their male coworkers," and they write about how this has a tie-in to self-efficacy.[2] There are certainly external factors influencing that report, but the buck for changing that starts with you. So many women tell me they don't have the time and are too busy to go to a leadership development training program, that they just want to focus on getting their work done because that is what will get results. At first I got so frustrated with this that I was speechless. Now I have a retort that gets their attention. I ask them how many times they have seen their male colleagues miss a round of golf so that they could get through their work queue. Invariably the answer is, "Never." The work waits and the round of golf is not missed. It's not missed because that is where some of that crucial leadership development, networking, and positioning for future business and career roles is taking place. I tell women they need to start thinking of their leadership development time as their round of golf—not to be missed. Sitting at your desk and plowing through work may have gotten you to where you are today, but it's not going to support you in your risk taking to move into new and different roles in the future.

Continue to invest in your ongoing education. Bindu chose to complete an Executive MBA after nearly twenty-one years of working and reaching a fairly senior position. She spoke passionately about this. "Most women don't stay vested in their careers by investing in their education, re-education, learning…It is absolutely essential that you are constantly refreshing your skills, learning new skills, and [that you] keep yourself open to new experiences. If there is a new interesting opportunity and it is risky, you are that much more comfortable taking it if you have a strong educational background to fall back on."

Do your homework but forget about checking all the boxes.

In the last chapter we heard Connie say, "I am not saying all women, but we think we have to know everything before we move into a new role, we have to check all the boxes and we know that is not realistic or even what is considered." So forget about checking all the boxes. But that doesn't mean you shouldn't ask some good questions and do your homework to know where you do stand in terms of your readiness to handle the risk of moving into and succeeding in your new role.

Debbie contributed, "I've learned there are so many ways to prepare for a new role you know nothing about. Every time I stepped into a role I've figured out every piece of literature I can read about it—

everything internally and externally. Reports, metrics, really do your homework so you feel more equipped to step into the role and be on a path to success." Janet emphasized not being afraid of asking questions, commenting that if you have a question, someone else in the room is likely to have one too. She said, "I've been told so many times, 'Wow, you're really not afraid to ask those stupid questions.' I do ask questions that are really simple. But it's not that sort of 'You should have known that' question. I have enough confidence in my own intellectual capability to realize I'm not being ridiculous if I don't know that thing. Just organize your thoughts to ask what you need to know in the right sequence so you are learning in an orderly way. People always appreciate that. If you're asking an orderly set of questions to clarify things and learn things, probably even the most sophisticated thinkers in the room are getting something out of your questions."

There are of course the fundamental questions, such as "What is the worst that can happen?" and "Will I be fired if it doesn't work?" Then there are questions to be asked around expectations. Connie advises asking expectations-related questions around technical outcomes, sales goals, and financial metrics. Leslie advises that expectations questions will help you feel good about making progress, especially if it is a blank-page type of role that has not existed in the organization before. For example, "What does success or what do successful steps look like? How will I know I am accomplishing whatever it is I am setting out to do?" Erin chimed in with other expectations questions—some strategic and some more tactical in nature. For example, "Why was this job formed? What is the goal of the role? What is the salary progression? What are the things you have to do to keep moving forward? What is the timeline for the role? Is this a career role or a stepping-stone to leadership or to the next opportunity? What is the travel expectation? What is the expectation of time away from the office? What is the reporting structure?" Jennifer brought up the necessity of asking what types of support structure and resources will be available to you—for example, additional team members or consultants.

There is homework to be done on the impact of this role on people—you and others. Connie recommends ensuring that you know your team, that you develop the relationships with the people who are either working for or with you, and that there is a clear understanding of the expectations of that team. She commented, "Strong relationships have been a theme of my work and how I manage risk. When we develop strong relationships, people are more willing to assist and more willing to invest in the success of the whole and not just in me as an individual." Leslie stressed the importance of understanding the impact of the role on you personally—does it add more stress, more hours, more pay, and more responsibility? She pointed out that many of these questions apply to any role, but with a blank-page type of role, the answers could well be a whole lot more nebulous.

Put the right support structures in place.

It's a lot easier to take risk when you aren't trying to do it alone. Put the right support structures in place and manage them carefully to support you in your calculated risk taking of moving into a new role. Maureen learned how the absence of advocates was hurting her when she first tried to make Partner at Lettuce Entertain You. She made sure that all changed when they asked her to come back, and she is now a Partner there. Wayne shared that at BDO they assign each of the female Partners and Senior Managers someone who can help them get to the next level, be a confidant, provide guidance, and watch their back. Tony advocates identifying men to be part of your sounding-board support structure, and how important it is for men to be willing to be a sounding board to their female colleagues that are taking calculated risks by moving into new roles.

Tony also brought up the importance of understanding who the stakeholders are in that new role and ensuring there is ample communication with them to increase the likelihood of success in your new role. Leveraging her belief that women tend to be collaborative learners, Leslie shared a technique she has used successfully for this. "When I started working in my most recent blank-sheet-of-paper job,

I drew out a grid of the people that I thought would be the most important for helping me gain some knowledge and understand a little bit more how to define the picture of what the role should be, and what my relationship with those people was like. What I found was that I had some people that I thought were very important, yet I didn't have a good relationship with them. So then I had to build to the point where I would be able to get them to assist in some way." Jennifer also gave some advice on working with the stakeholders in your new role. "Identify those key stakeholders very early and talk with them very quickly to understand what their objectives are and what their views are. Understand and set up clear dates, milestones, and objectives. If those aren't clear, decisions and timeframes can linger on and spin...Lay out very clearly what are the success factors and what are the guiding principles we need that we're just going to align on all the time because they matter. We're always going to come back to these every time we make a decision. It keeps us in the goalposts."

Nancy Mueller shared the consequences of underestimating the extent of change when moving from one role to another within your current organization and not being deliberate in building a new change network. She learned that lesson when she transitioned from the Chief Actuary role to the COO role. Nine months later she recognized how different the skills were, and how she would have benefited from being more purposeful in her connections. "When it's progressive in the same place and everyone around the table knows you, while I think that folks were there to help me, I didn't even recognize it in myself that it's really different. You're going to the same office, driving to the same office. So much is the same. So you have to create a 'this is different' and change your routine...I had an informal network of mentors, but that was a continuation. [In hindsight] I would have changed mentors rather than continuing with the same network and communication structure. It was like nine months later that I recognized [this], and then I connected with a sounding board. It was not so much a mentor [as] 'I need help, this is what I'm thinking, does this make sense,' a good sounding board.

Things had gotten up to speed, and things were starting to work, and I felt like, 'Geez, if I had recognized what a big change this was, it wouldn't have taken me nine months.' But you're in the middle of it. You don't realize how hard it is when you're in the middle of it."

Prepare for many options and outcomes.

There are no guarantees when taking risk. You can and should prepare as much as is reasonable for a new role, but at some point you have to stop preparing and just do it. As you navigate your way into and through this new role you have taken on, prepare for many options and outcomes. Debbie wisely said, "Prepare for many outcomes, including failure. That's something that I think that women—and maybe people in general—don't do enough when they are taking risk. People get so invested in the risk they've taken, the path they've taken, the opportunity they've been given. They don't prepare for the what-if options and the outcomes that may not be optimal, including failure. What's the backup plan if this doesn't work? How are you going to manage that?" Debbie is not saying you will fail. What she is saying is to prepare for an outcome that might be different from what you and others originally envisioned. Success is superb, but ensure that at a minimum you know the broad constructs of your go-to strategy if you hit bumps in the road. This is relevant preparation for your role diversification.

The first aspect of preparing for many options and outcomes is to be realistic about your learning curve in the new role. If there is a lot of new stuff, it's going to take time to take it all in and figure it out. Recall Janet's comments in the last chapter about renewing capabilities. She built on that, saying, "The whole activity of renewing means that you're going in to do something where you have no reason to believe you're going to do it extremely competently at the beginning. So you have to be confident enough in your core that when you're not performing like a top performer in that very new thing, you accept that you're learning, that you're junior for a while. That's so important. Having that kind of nervous fear that you're not at the top of your [game] for that particular skill set that you're doing is a really healthy emotion to occasionally have. It keeps you sharp, on top of your game."

The second aspect of preparing for many options and outcomes is to be willing to put aside some norms. Jennifer described her situation when she left Accenture to work for Zurich North America. "We also made the decision at that point that my husband would stay home and take care of the family. We looked at it as a business decision. We put everything on paper and we said this is what makes the most sense. That was the point where we made the family decision that I was going to have more of the career trajectory. We did that on purpose because it made logical economic sense and sort of threw away some of the norms. The other piece that's a little bit interesting is that my husband is the firstborn son in a Korean family. This also adds complexity where he's expected to be—cultural expectations—the one that should be taking care of the family, making the money, and we flipped it all on its head. So it was a big risk in terms of our families and the cultural norms. But I felt that I could, because we made that decision together. We were very aligned, and I knew that I had his support and confidence at home. So we did it." Nancy Mueller's husband took on the role of primary household caregiver when she took the job with Zurich North America and they moved to Chicago. Annette's husband did the same when she moved to the United States with Aviva. Vlada put some cultural norms aside when she left Russia as a single mother with her baby to be the Executive Assistant to the global leader of BP's Lubricants business. All of these women had their share of challenges along the way as they put some norms aside, but they do provide role models for other women who may want to make similar choices.

The third aspect of preparing for many options and outcomes is to realize that quite simply, you always have options. Jennifer and Leslie took on unchartered roles without being concerned about what would follow—they knew they were valued employees and would always have options. After about six years in HR, during a reorganization—knowing they were going to drop one of the people in the HR Business Partner role—Annette voluntarily stepped away from her

HR Business Partner role. She didn't yet have plan B, but it felt right, and she certainly knew she had options. She ended up being offered a newly created role to lead up talent management for the whole of Aviva UK. Yanyan, Jan, and Melanie are just some of the entrepreneurs in this book—giving it their best shot and knowing they will end up feet first no matter what. Mukta and Vlada are just some of the people you've heard from that have packed up their entire lives and moved across continents, knowing that no matter where they hang their hat and call home, they will always have options. After moving continents, working in the large corporate setting, starting my own businesses, building new programs, and now taking another risk in taking the better part of six months off to write this book—even on the tough days I too remind myself, and I do believe, that I will always have options. As you do, and as you always will.

Chapter 11 Notes

1   Ely, Robin J., Herminia Ibarra, and Deborah Kolb. "Taking Gender Into Account: Theory and Design for Women's Leadership Development Programs." *Academy of Management and Learning Education* 10, no. 3 (2011): 485.

2   McCormick, Michael J., Jesús Tanguma, and Anita Sohn López-Forment. "Gender Differences in Beliefs about Leadership Capabilities: Exploring the Glass Ceiling Phenomenon with Self-Efficacy Theory." *Kravis Leadership Institute Leadership Review* (Spring 2003): 4.

Chapter 12: Perspectives on Resilience and Power

Yanyan learned resilience from her grandmother, who turned one hundred years old this year. Her grandmother still maintains a traditional Chinese lifestyle and lives in their home village. Yanyan's grandmother was twenty years old when she was married; her husband was seven years old. In the era of Chinese feudalism, women had no power. In her one hundred years she's survived wars, invaders, and the Cultural Revolution. She still lives by herself and cooks dumplings for Yanyan when she visits. She never says "Yes" or "No"; she just tries her best to share her wisdom. Yanyan said, "Resilience is actually power."

Bindu told the story of her great-grandmother, who lost a son. She had taken him to a nearby village for a fair and he died there. In India it is traditionally the man in the family who performs the last rites. Based on the circumstances, her great-grandmother performed them and then returned home bearing the sad news. Bindu's great-grandfather died at the young age of twenty-five. Her great-grandmother set up a small hotel eatery to support herself and her sole surviving child—her daughter (Bindu's grandmother). Bindu's grandmother had eighteen children. Her great-grandmother was around for the better part of the first ten children's youth. Bindu said of her great-grandmother, "She didn't sit around and mope about what life had dealt to her. She just went about doing what needed doing." Bindu's mother-in-law had her own challenges. She lost her mother when she was seven. She continued her schooling, made sure her sisters got educated, got married, had five children, lost two of them, and lived through Bindu and her husband's business challenges. Bindu said, "She didn't lose her smile through all of that. She would say, 'Sure, if that's happened, it's happened. Let's see how we can come out of this.' " Bindu commented, "I always think of resilience as being something that women are born with."

Who do you draw your resilience from? Do you know all your family's stories? As you peruse the images in your family photo album and see those smiling faces and stern countenances staring back at you, can you identify who you've inherited your resilient characteristics from? There is no doubt you have it in you. There is no doubt that you can be and are resilient. That is excellent because by its nature risk taking requires resilience. The more you take risks the more likely it is that you'll have to draw on your resilience. Unplanned events will come around the corner, surprises will yank you out of your comfort zone, missteps will occur, and there will be bumps and bruises along the way. To get to the other side of your calculated risk taking, to get to success, resilience is mandatory. Resilience is what will help you get through this risk and the next one and the one after that. Resilience keeps you signing up for more risks so you can realize your full potential. Resilience is how you bounce back when things don't go as planned. It gets you to raise your head, take a deep breath, change your approach, put yesterday behind you and today in front of you, and utter a warrior's roar of "Attack." Resilience reinforces your belief that the risk was worth taking, that you will prevail, and that you will succeed; it keeps you aligned with your passion and purpose. Resilience is required!

Recognize there is no going backwards. Nancy Sharp's mother raised six children on her own after her husband died. Nancy was twelve years old at the time and the eldest child. When Nancy's husband died in 2010 she took her cues from her mom. "My mom— being a great role model and a widow—said, 'Nan, you only have a couple of choices. Stay home and in bed or get out the front door and do something.' You have to go through all those stages to get out the door. What an opportunity lost not to get out the door and smell the sunshine and develop yourself to be all you can be."

Manage your own expectations. Karen advises, "If you're not anticipating the additional toll that operating in a different environment can take, you're not going to be as resilient as you would be otherwise. In some ways it's about managing your own expectations and managing what you anticipate it will take to deliver a project, manage a business, deliver a solution, whatever the outcome is. If you go in underestimating what it's going to take to be successful, then the chances are you'll be less resilient front and center. If you have had that conversation with yourself and you are expecting it, your resilience is enhanced tremendously. That it will not be a linear progression of success to success to success. That challenges and difficulties will come along the way, and what doesn't kill you will make you stronger."

Take into account your track record with endurance and success when taking risks. Focus on what you can control and move forward. Cathy teaches us to look within ourselves to find the wherewithal to move on. She recommends asking yourself two questions. "I might look back to a prior success and say, 'Have I endured and succeeded before?' Therefore as dark as it may look this second, has my resilience and fortitude paid off before? If so then I ought to have faith that it will [again] if I conduct myself in the same way. You can draw on success...You do have to stop and say, 'Is what I am focused on right now something I can control or can't control?' Because we very much want to control all of it. You have to make a very conscious decision whether you can influence that which you are spending your time thinking about or obsessing with or staying awake over. You need to very cognitively move away from the things you can't control and move away from the past. We move from where we are. There is no purpose in yesterday unless there is a lesson to be learned. You can't go back. You can only move forward."

Celebrate the learning and take an outside-in view. Francene told me, "A resilient woman is OK if it's not the fast route—the route of the hare. The tortoise route may be OK if I have challenges and I learn. I call it 'celebrate the learning.' If that doesn't work, then let me explore and go to my network to find different ways to do it... Some things will be successful. Some will not. We're going to celebrate the learnings." Annette spoke about taking an outside-in view. "Watching yourself as you're going through it. I've learned over time to take everything I do as a learning opportunity. I always take that step back. What am I getting out of this? What am I learning from this? What could I do differently because of this? Would I do this again, or would I take a different route, or am I comfortable with what I've done? Be much more self-aware and know when I need to draw on my resilience, or when I need to pull on networks, or when I need to call out for help."

Have a support network around you. You will need to draw on different people in your network in different capacities over time—sometimes as a cheerleader, sometimes as a coach or advisor or mentor or ally, sometimes as a sponsor, sometimes as a friend, and sometimes as a venting outlet. Annette drew out a relationship map when she made her transition from the United Kingdom to the United States. Mapping out who she knew in what capacity and how they could be an ally to her during the transition period and beyond made the whole transition seems less daunting—it increased her resilience. Connie spoke about faith and friends. "I am a woman for whom faith is my anchor. So everything about my life and the way I approach things is based on my Christian faith. For me, my faith is that place where through prayer and meditation, I can go to replenish and refocus. Having a prayer circle of a few women where we talk about what issues are concerning us. We allow our faith to strengthen us. I have so many wonderful people supporting me that I sometimes say, 'I can fall down without falling apart.' I have a group of trusted confidants with whom I have a profound level of trust, and a profound level of transparency."

Stop blaming yourself and don't take it personally. Cathy reflected, "Maybe on average it's more likely men think it wasn't their fault. I heard a good story from a soccer coach one day who said, 'It's entirely different coaching girls from coaching boys. When you are coaching you may stand in front of the team and say, 'That was the worst display of soccer I have ever seen; I have never seen the team play so poorly.' All the girls are sitting there thinking, 'I believe he's talking about me and I should probably just quit because he's not going to invite me back to the next game.' The guys are just elbowing the kid next to him, saying, 'Buddy, I'm pretty sure he's talking about you.' So I think resilience might come from inherent self-confidence that if it didn't go right it's probably not my fault." Roger drew the contrast between the male who tends to be more transactional, typically takes things less personally, walks away with one or two scars from a tough situation, and brushes it all off fairly easily, compared to the female, who becomes more attached to the situation, internalizes what went wrong, and finds it harder to put it all aside, let go, and move on.

I subscribe to all of the above. Here are some more powerful strategies that are part of how I operate. **Get some exercise.** There is nothing like fresh air, physical exertion, and sweat to clean out the noise in your head and the hurt in your heart and get those goal-oriented juices flowing again. **Get sad, then mad, then bad.** It's OK to give yourself some time to feel down and lick your wounds. Then allow yourself to get angry in private so you can vent your frustrations. Tell yourself again all the reasons why you must move forward. Then come back out of the gate in full force—re-energized, refocused, recommitted, and unstoppable. **Be creative and innovative.** There are always options and alternatives—other ways to get things done and move closer to the endgame. The ways and means you first identified are likely not how it will actually happen, so constantly ask yourself how else you can get there. **Be open to an end state that is different from what you first envisioned.** Have room to flex, adapt, and grow as you move forward. This is not about sacrificing your vision or your ideals. It's about achieving them by understanding that there is more than one form in which they can come to fruition. Your challenge and opportunity is to end with the form that is most likely to yield success. **Be willing to be vulnerable.** Being resilient is not about being the nut that is impossible to crack or the façade that makes everything appear perfect every hour of every day. We are human, and taking risks is tough on us. By being vulnerable you allow yourself to be open to inputs from others and to inspiration from a multitude of sources. Manage your vulnerability and don't let it dominate, but welcome its presence in your life every now and again.

Resilience is required if you want to take risks. So is power. As you bolster your resilience, you are indeed fortifying an important source of your own power. To be an effective risk taker, you have to be willing and able to recognize and use power appropriately. Let's now transition to perspectives on power in the context of women taking calculated career risks. Irrespective of gender, many people feel uncomfortable when the subject of power comes up, and unfortunately many conversations about women and power veer off into negative territory. Power is neither a bad word nor something to be shied away from. When it comes to risk taking during your career, we must spend time on this topic. If you are going to risk, you must have an appreciation of what power means to you and how to utilize it effectively. There are many nuances to power. Power is your ability to achieve a specific outcome for which you are risking in the first place. Power is realizing your potential. Power is being comfortable with who you are and getting others comfortable with that as well. Power is the ability to exert control when necessary as you navigate through your risk taking. Power is how you get along with others, how you influence people, how you risk with other people. When taking risk, persistence is power and integrity is power. Power is about what you can do to aid others in their risk taking.

When taking risks in your career, you need to be clear about what power you do have and what your sources of power are. The obvious sources are things like the position you hold and the authority that comes with that, your network and alliances you have built, and your performance record, both as a leader and in terms of delivering business results. Not-so-obvious sources of power are how effectively you leverage your emotional intelligence, the amount of trust that people place in you, and establishing some degree of financial independence for yourself. Everything you have learned in the prior chapters and how you apply it adds to your power and expands your sources of power when taking risks. What comes next is using your power. Here are perspectives to aid you in using your power effectively in your risk taking.

Use your power to find the right answer. Debbie commented, "The best leaders I have ever seen, male or female—and I would say this is a common trait of successful leaders—they are well aware they are not the one with all the answers. In fact, the higher you go in an organization, the less likely you are to have all the answers. The skill you need to develop is the ability to know the right answer when you see it."

Use your power to organize thoughts, lead the decision-making process, and drive change. Recall Janet's insights about driving risky decisions, leading the development of decision-making frameworks, and leading people to a clear and rational decision. Connie extended this into using your power to drive change, saying, "I have known women who had no title and very little education, but they were powerful because they were able to organize themselves and their thoughts around a specific issue in such a way that they could not and would not be ignored. There are women throughout history that started huge movements. These were women who, based on political and other issues of the day, would have been viewed as powerless. But they were able to gather their personal power and formulate a specific request, demand, or movement, and it has changed our world in so many ways."

Use your power to bring calm and restore order whilst still maintaining direction and focus. It is to be expected that during the course of risk taking there will be periods where uncertainty is rampant, as stakeholders affect outcomes, tensions are high, and the path forward is unclear. Getting beyond this requires drawing on your power to sail the choppy seas while still keeping a laser focus on getting to the clear and calm waters ahead. Roger advises to first off find your own inner calm to draw on, disengaging for a short time if necessary to gather your thoughts. Then understand as much as possible where others are coming from and find appropriate alternative ways to re-engage with your stakeholders.

Use your power to collaborate and be inclusive but to ultimately own decisions and move forward. Debbie and Bindu both commented on this one. Debbie said, "Collaboration does not mean consensus building. That's the bold line that we need to be careful about. Collaboration is about not overdeliberating but getting at the answers, getting all the opinions on the table, and getting them pretty quickly, and then being decisive. It's helping people to understand why you've made the decision you have. It's being decisive and moving on—recognizing when you have seen and heard the right answer, and explaining it and making the decision and moving forward. That's bold leadership. It's not a weakness to have listened to others, drawn out opinions, explored options." Bindu added to this, saying, "When being inclusive, make it very clear that is a strength, it is not a weakness. Don't allow someone to walk all over you just because you're asking for their ideas or their opinions." Another element to consider here is when sharing your power, take care to not let it be diminished. Connie commented, "Sharing power without your own power diminishing is critical from a woman's perspective, because we are judged and evaluated differently in leadership roles. While I might be willing to share power with a very alpha male, it is important to ensure that it is not construed in a way that he gets all the credit, or the perception is that I did not do anything to benefit the outcome. As to the notion of sharing power—yes, when it is necessary. But when I am in charge of it, I am in charge of it. I own it. I cover all the ground I stand on. Role definition is very important."

Use your power to handle opposing forces. Risk taking by its nature implies that you will encounter opposing forces in some fashion and from one source or another along the way. Connie mentioned three types of opposing forces. "From my experience being in corporate, there is passive-aggressive behavior, there is outright aggressive behavior, and then there is benign neglect. Benign neglect is where I might need additional information or course correction, and nothing is said, then watching something go off the rails. There is the aggressive, in-your-face approach, which says 'I do not believe that you are capable of doing this' or 'I am not going to help you' or 'I quite frankly want you to fail, because I do not believe you belong here.' Then there are the people who will drop negative statements in your lap or make it difficult to achieve an outcome." She advised using the skill of discernment to be able to understand where people are coming from by listening carefully and having a strong and expansive network of people who have your back and are helping you to spot opposition early and prepare to deal with it.

Use your power to exert influence in your own unique and authentic way. Your ability to get people on board and supporting the risk is an important factor in ultimate success with risk taking. Use your power to get to the table, to get the ear of key stakeholders, and to influence others. Cathy calls it "quiet power." She talks about being aware of how the game is being played but not necessarily playing it the way it is being played. "You can't do things with only your style, unaware of what the political realities are, what the corporate culture is, what the rules of the game are. Maybe there are boy's rules or old rules or power rules or whatever there are. You've got to be aware, but you can't conform 100 percent, because I think we [women] do on average bring a different style and our organizations deserve to benefit from it."

Use your power to prioritize and say "no" more often. Taking risk requires laser focus in order to be successful at it. You can't be juggling too many things at once. Connie likes the concept of having a prioritization list as opposed to a to-do list. She also subscribes strongly to saying "no" more often. She recognizes that controlling what she says "no" to is a source of power for her. She said, "We give too much because of the expectations we have of ourselves and [expectations] that others have of us. It is not always achievable in a way that allows you to be successful and true to yourself. We are human beings, not human doings." She encourages you to acknowledge if saying "yes" all the time is feeding something in your ego, find a way to let that go, and coach and delegate to others.

These are some ways in which you can and should use your power when taking calculated risks in your career. Be conscious about the use of power and its impact during your risk taking. Overuse and misuse of power by anyone—male or female—can alienate others and diminish your effectiveness during risk taking. Women have to be particularly tuned into this, as unfortunately in some cases we are still held to different standards. That may not be fair, but it is reality. Tony commented on differences he has observed regarding men and women and use of power in risk taking. "For male counterparts, risk taking has been seen forever as a standard piece of an executive or somebody in any type of role, just part of their every day. Women have been seen much more in a non-risk taker role; therefore when they take the risks, the way in which they take those risks is in some cases very clear, evident, and bold, and that may create some tension in the organization. I think that is driven primarily by the environment, in just trying to break in and establish themselves." Tony shared how he has seen very smart and capable individuals impact their ability to be successful in their risk taking by how they utilize their power, and that this can impact women in particular. "Again, I think it's the culture of women in the workplace. We are trying to get at parity. That is a lot of hard work. Working towards that parity, at times the overuse of power tends to deflect on their [women's] effectiveness in taking risks, or it tends to in some cases magnify the risk taking."

The more you increase your awareness and knowledge about resilience and power, the more effective you will be at incorporating them into your approach to risk taking during your career. I highly recommend the following as starting resources.

In a 2010 *Harvard Business Review* article, "How to Bounce Back from Adversity," Joshua D. Margolis and Paul G. Stoltz identify four lenses through which managers can view adverse events to help them shift from cause-oriented thinking to response-oriented thinking and subsequently take action and move forward. The four lenses are control, impact, breadth, and duration. The authors then describe a resilience regimen—a series of pointed questions to help you reframe negative events in productive ways. Three specific types of questions are used to help you shift your thinking from reflexive thinking to active thinking—specifying questions, visualizing questions, and collaborating questions. Examples of each type of question are included for each of the four lenses.[1] I find it to be a very practical and insightful regimen that you can apply to anything from your simplest pain point to your most complex issue requiring all the resilience you can muster.

Diane Coutu's *Harvard Business Review* piece "How Resilience Works" covers three practices you can use to help cultivate your resilience: face down reality, search for meaning, and continually improvise and be inventive.[2] Granted it is a more introspective and abstract approach than the one mentioned above, but you will need aspects of both to truly strengthen your capacity for resilience. Without the level of introspection that this article advises, I doubt you will be honest enough with yourself or challenge yourself enough to get the full benefit of the other regimen.

It is important to acknowledge the role that confidence plays in building resilience. As such you should also take advantage of resources that focus on confidence. In part of Katty Jay and Claire Shipman's 2014 book *The Confidence Code*, the authors look at how you can choose to become more confident by taking action and courting risk, and how those actions change your physical wiring.[3]

On the subject of women and power, I highly recommend "Gender, emotion and power in work relationships," an article by Belle Rose Ragins and Doan E. Winkel that appeared in a 2011 issue of *Human Resource Management Review*. In this paper the authors examine how gender and emotion combine to influence the development of power in work relationships.[4] It would be impossible to risk without emotion, so the relationship between gender, emotion, and power in work relationships has bearing on the risks you take in your career.

Chapter 12 Notes

1   Margolis, Joshua D., and Stoltz, Paul G. "How to Bounce Back from Adversity." *Harvard Business Review* (January–February 2010, reprint): 1–7.

2   Coutu, Diane L. "How Resilience Works." *Harvard Business Review* (May 2002, reprint): 1–8.

3   Kay, Katty, and Shipman, Claire. *The Confidence Code.* HarperBusiness, 2014.

4   Ragins, Belle Rose, and Winkel, Doan E. "Gender, emotion and power in work relationships." *Human Resource Management Review* 21 (2011): 377–393.

Chapter 13: The Joy of Rescuing Yourself and Celebrating Yourself

Stepping into the universe of risk taking means you will experience successes and failures, excitement and fear, joy and sadness, rises and falls. Risk taking is a rollercoaster with twists and turns, ups and downs. Risk taking is a maze with dead ends and light at the end of the tunnel. Risk taking is a journey. Your willingness to take calculated risks during your career means you have decided to write your own travelogue, your own guidebook, and not simply pick up someone else's. Each time you take another calculated risk in your career journey, you will have many opportunities to celebrate your arrival at key milestones and successes. There will also be times when you experience a failure and you need to rescue yourself, because this is your journey and you own it. Rescuing yourself is as important as celebrating yourself and is both joyous and wonderful. Your ability to rescue yourself stems from you defining what success means to you and what failure means to you, and not letting anyone else define for you or impose on you what those terms mean. It stems from your ability to embrace and learn from both your successes and your failures. When you risk and succeed, challenge yourself to reflect and learn to be even more effective next time around. When you risk and fail, make it intelligent failure and learn from it. Use both success and intelligent failure to rescue yourself during your risk taking.

There are reasons why you don't learn as much from successes as you do from failures. In "Why Leaders Don't Learn From Success," Francesca Gino and Gary P. Pisano discuss three interrelated impediments to learning from success: fundamental attribution errors, overconfidence bias, and failure-to-ask-why syndrome. With fundamental attribution errors, the authors state in this *Harvard Business Review* piece that, "When we succeed, we're likely to conclude that our talents and our current model or strategy are the reasons. We also give short shrift to the part that environmental factors and random events may have played."[1] In the case of someone else's success, we tend to do the reverse—ascribe it more to the environment and random events and less so to their skills and strategy. In the case of our own failure, we tend to ascribe it to the environment and random events and not to any lack of our skills and strategy. On the impediment of overconfidence bias, while you certainly need confidence to take risks, too much of it can be a problem, and success can make us believe we are better decision makers than we actually are. In terms of failing to ask why, "Success is commonly interpreted as evidence not only that your existing strategy and practices work but also that you have all the knowledge and information you need."[1] That may not actually be the case, but success makes us less reflective. The authors advise actively countering these impediments by celebrating your successes but still examining them, and by systematically reviewing your approach and techniques to not only find ways to further improve but also to keep experimenting and trying out new things that may work even better. They point out identifying the appropriate time frame to evaluate your performance, because if you're off with your timing, you might misconstrue which factors contributed to your success or failure.[1] To be a successful serial risk taker during your career, strengthen your likelihood of success and your ability to rescue yourself by not falling prey to impeding behaviors brought on by success.

Just because something doesn't work out doesn't mean that you are a failure. Your intelligent failure can be a great asset in how you rescue yourself in future risk-taking efforts if you take the opportunity to learn and discover new ways of moving forward. Most important of all—don't give up, just get back up and keep on trying and experimenting. You'll improve your odds of success if you make more tries. Now let's take a look at specific ways in which you can leverage intelligent failure to rescue yourself during your risk taking.

Decide what success and failure look like before you begin, and identify markers that will help you recognize which track you are on. Partial success is still success. Partial failure if you recognize it soon enough enables you to rescue yourself, because you can course-correct and get back on track towards success with the risk you took. Diane embraces this philosophy. "There are things along the way that can give you hints if you are getting there. So set those up first. Come up with experiments. Set points along the way before you would get to success or failure so that early on you can figure out if this is going off course or it's not what you thought, and you can either adapt or bail."

Test your assumptions. When you took the risk you made certain assumptions. Whether you are encountering success or failure, make sure to test your assumptions and be willing to learn as you do so. Tested assumptions can help you attain greater success with your risk as your move forward and help prevent future failure. In the first year of my gen-xyb™ High Tea program, in addition to having the program participants, at each session I also invited guests. The shifting guests provided the program participants additional networking opportunities and different perspectives, and they also kept the energy level up throughout the yearlong program by changing who was present at the sessions. I assumed this was working great for everyone because people always raved about who they met. After the first year of the program wrapped up, I received some additional feedback that made me test that assumption. I ended up changing the program for the second year—setting aside some sessions where no additional guests would be present; they would be closed sessions for the program participants only. I am still risking with continuing to push forward with and build this new program in the marketplace, and testing that assumption allowed me to learn and rescue myself in that aspect of year two of the program instead of blindly continuing on with my original plan.

Don't be clouded by your passion. It's natural that you are passionate about your risk. If you weren't, it is unlikely you would have taken the risk in the first place. The challenge is to not let yourself get clouded by your passion, because if you do it makes it tougher to rescue yourself and others. Kim's passion and her job is opening doors for women-owned and minority-owned vendors in corporate America by having them be part of deals structured by larger service providers. Kim told me about a situation where she had pushed hard for a particular minority-owned vendor to be part of a deal structure, but her passion for the cause clouded her ability to see some issues. She continued to receive pushback from her colleagues about this particular vendor, but she initially discounted the pushback and attributed it to bias. Then it blew up. Kim elaborated, "Then I was forced to take an honest and objective look at these two parties. Even if you're passionate, even if you are making these assumptions and looking at it with rose-colored glasses, there might be some validity as to why this situation isn't going to work. You need to be willing to say 'OK, I was wrong.' I've learned some pretty hard lessons based on values, assumptions, and taking sides on what I believe to be right and wrong." Roger observed how the passion for what we are risking on may lead many women to have a tougher time relinquishing the emotional attachment to the risk we have invested in, but how imperative it is to recognize when it is necessary to do so.

Fail fast, fail forward, and minimize the cost of failure. When you take a risk it's better to find out sooner rather than later whether you're headed towards success or not. You'll be in a better position to identify the root cause of a problem if you can narrow the time frame from initiation to going off course, and the quicker you can correct course, the sooner you'll head towards success. That's failing fast and failing forward. There's another dimension to this—failing and course-correcting as cheaply as possible in terms of both financial and emotional investments. Katie commented, "We have a small company. We have a fail-fast mentality. So throw everything you can into it, keep optimizing, then if you find that's not working, take a step back, figure out a new way to do it, and then run with a new way...I am lucky that I am in a culture that embraces frequent feedback. I don't have to wait until something is done to know if something was a success or a failure. We are always working together to make sure that something is done in the best way, which I think is probably very unique; I don't think that happens in every company." When I first started working on concepts for programs around development and advancement of women in the workplace, I formulated a vision and program outline that turned out to be far too broad and generic in nature. No one in the marketplace was biting. Based on the feedback, I quickly returned to the drawing board and totally refocused my efforts, ultimately developing the gen-xyb™ High Tea concept, which is proving to be very successful. That was a classic case of rescuing myself by failing fast with minimal cost and failing forward by being able to course-correct into success.

Manage your self-talk. The encouragement you get from yourself and others when you have success with your risk taking lifts you up and away. When things don't go as planned, you have to deal with everything you hear from others as well as your own internal voices of self-doubt and worry. You have to manage your self-talk to be able to rescue yourself and get back on track with your risk taking. Melinda likes to tackle head-on key questions that typically arise: What's the worst case if you abandon this and move on to something else? What are you afraid of? What if you can't find another job? Her advice is if your risk was taking a new job or role and it hasn't panned out, you have to believe that if you found this one you can find another one. She also stressed that it is OK to tell people if you made a mistake by taking on your current position. What's important in that situation is to be clear as to what it is about your situation now that you don't like and to make others comfortable that you understand that well enough and know how you would evaluate it differently to avoid doing it twice in a row—that you have learned from it and are ready to move on. Melinda also wants you to remember that not only do you have all the same skills and experience that you had when you came to your current job, but you've now added to that. You are more valuable than you were before, so what makes you think nobody else will recognize that? Connie shared her self-talk. "When I have done something less than spectacular, the language I have is, 'Well, Connie, you failed pretty well that time. How are you going to do it differently?' All of us have self-talk. It's how we speak to ourselves in the good times and in the not-so-good times. I am very mindful of what I'm saying to myself internally, no matter what it is. How am I treating me? Because if I do not honor myself and treat myself with great love and respect, there is no way I can give that to other people."

Be willing to say "stop". You are at the center of your calculated risk taking. Only you can make the final judgment call as to whether you should keep moving forward with your risk or not. Only you can decide if the time is right or if you need to chart another course. There is no shame in making a call on timing or in charting a new course. These strategies are part of how you rescue yourself and preserve yourself for future risk taking. When I first left Deloitte, many people encouraged me to start my own company right away. I was still getting over the risk and change of just leaving Deloitte. I told people to stop pressuring me, that the time was not right. I spent the next eighteen months at Aon, during which I preserved myself and prepared myself for my next risk. When I left Aon, that was when I started my own company—when the time was right for me.

Be proud of your scrap heap and make it part of your story. Everyone has stuff that happens, risks they take in their career that don't work out well. Your ability to rescue yourself isn't just about what you learn and take away from those experiences to make you better at risk taking in the future. It's also about how to embrace those experiences, take pride in them, and reflect them in your story about your risk-taking journey. Rescue yourself by using those experiences and lessons learned in your story to help others understand why they should risk on you or for you or with you, and why you're going to achieve ultimate success. The memorable stories we have heard throughout this book are part of the scrap heaps of our wonderful cast of characters in this book. What's in your scrap heap?

So now you've rescued yourself and you have continued on with your calculated risk taking. Success will indeed come your way. It will come in a multitude of ways that provide satisfaction and fulfillment on many different fronts. In celebrating your successes you will also rightly be celebrating yourself for having the courage and fortitude to risk in the first place. Celebrate you must, because immersing yourself in the joy of those moments will provide nourishment and sustenance in your future risk taking endeavors. Risk looks and feels different for each person; each person defines what successful outcomes are for themselves in the context of their risk taking in their own unique way. They are all wonderful.

Francene's definition of success when taking risk is all about alignment between her career and her vision for her life. "You are responsible for your own life and your own happiness and what you achieve." For Yanyan, if she takes a risk and as a result she sees herself starting to change, that's success right there. "As soon as you start to change, the risk—the adventure—is already a success. Then you can feel you are a lot happier and a lot more satisfied with your life. When you wake up every morning, you feel it is such a nice day and you feel so energetic to do the things you like. That is good success." Erin's definition of success with her risk taking incorporates how she is able to help and impact the people around her while at the same time advancing herself and her career. "My definition for success with myself when taking risks revolves around how I'm developing, what that trajectory looks like, and the steps that I'm taking to get there. But it also is equally important to me what I'm doing to help the people around me be successful." For Mukta, success is based on her ability to strike the right balance between what her family needs for their care and well-being and what she needs for her own personal well-being and career satisfaction. Mukta has had a very successful career with BP. A while back she made a decision to start working from home because her family needed her more. She understood that it would limit the types of roles available to her within BP for as long as she needed to be able to work from home. Mukta fights hard to not let other people's definition of success affect her. "But it's very natural to let it affect you because that is how society is. When you go out to a dinner party or cocktail party, the first thing they ask is, 'What do you do?' You know that by the moment you answer that question they will have made a judgment about who you are, where you are, what you are doing, and what kind of a person you are. So it does make a difference, but I have worked really hard on myself to say it does not influence how I take risks, because I will take risks when I am ready to take that risk."

Toni describes her definition of success: "Success to me is if I know when I've concluded that I've done the absolute most I could do, the best job I could ever deliver, and then tallying up what I've learned. Each adventure or each step has to give you some kind of growth. Whether it is knowledge or confidence or exposure or experience—those are all successful takeaways...I don't value the job title or the money as much as what I can contribute or impact. If I've contributed everything that I can, then I call that success." Leslie shared her view of success. "I want to leave any situation knowing that I'm better and it's better because I was there. So I'm always looking for the impact on me and on other people. When it comes to other people's definitions, quite frankly, I don't care. Because only if you're exactly walking in my shoes doing exactly what I'm doing can you be a judge of whether or not I'm successful. Now, having said that I understand that an organization has to have certain metrics by which they measure success, and I get that. But those metrics are not always the only way in which to measure success. There are times when there must be short-term setbacks in order to get something in the long term. If I'm having an impact on the short term even though I'm not meeting the metrics someplace else, I can still consider myself successful, because I believe that's the right step to take to get to what I need to in the long run. But I don't feel the job is done until I feel the job is done, and I don't measure success by what somebody else thinks is success. I measure it by what I think it is."

Sometimes as we get caught up in the pursuit of our dreams we get confused. We confuse failure with success, and success with failure. We get caught up in subscribing to other people's definitions of success and failure instead of staying true to our own. When we get caught up in that, we're likely to become afraid to risk again. We're likely to forget how to both rescue ourselves and celebrate ourselves in our own risk taking. Don't go there. It's not worth it. I have two stories to illustrate this.

Reflect back on Peg's story about finally leaving the big law firm she had been at for years and moving over to a smaller firm. At her old firm she got caught up in other people's definition of success—money and prestige. She said, "I felt like I wasn't successful. I felt like a failure.

I felt like I had worked really hard and done really good work, and wasn't valued. It made me doubt myself and really question whether or not I was a good lawyer." When she transitioned to the smaller law firm, she was worried about risking both prestige and money. But for a variety of reasons she felt it was worth making the change, and as it turns out, while she suspects she may have lost something in terms of prestige, she has certainly not taken a financial hit. At the smaller law firm she has had great success on both the professional front, as evidenced by her hours, billings, and expanded client base, and on the personal front, as evidenced by her and her son's recognition of how much happier she is.

She told me that one of the things that really helped reinforce that she was a good lawyer and a successful lawyer was the fact that every client that she had worked with at her old firm came with her to the new firm. One of her clients who was an in-house accountant for an insurance company called his in-house General Counsel in a panic because he thought Peg had a noncompete covenant that would prevent them from engaging her services at her new firm. His reaction was, "How are we going to get our work done without Peg?" He was relieved when he found out that was not the case. Peg said, "It was wonderful, because it was a real reinforcement. What I felt—and who knows if my perceptions were totally right, but they were at least to some extent right—I felt like I was being told by my old law firm that I'm not valuable, that I'm not a good lawyer, that I'm not successful. Then here I have this client saying, 'Oh, I thought for a panicked moment that we can't use you anymore, and I'm so glad to hear that we can.' So that was very helpful, especially after my son pointed out the difference in my voice. For a while there I used every excuse that I could to call people at the old firm and tell them the story. The one partner who made the comment to me, 'Well, you could be a valuable partner'—I do occasionally have daydreams about running into him at the train station and thanking him for being an agent of change in my life." Peg has recast and now subscribes to her own definition of success. "For me a risk is worth taking if it's going to fully engage all parts of me and is going to result in me growing...

So for me taking the risk of changing law firms has worked out economically, it has worked out as far as quality of work I am doing. But where it's really worked out has been allowing me to be fully me, and that has been just a wonderful gift."

The second story is my own story. I have always been a big-vision, big-goals, go-for-it person. I took you on a whirlwind tour of my life back in Chapter 1. You may recall that in 2007, in what came as a shock to many people—including myself—I decided to leave Deloitte in the year I was making my final run towards becoming a Partner. It was not a decision arrived at lightly. All the way back in my university years I aspired to work for a big global consulting firm and become a Partner. And 2007 was going to be the year that I achieved that goal! Here's the conundrum. The great thing about being a big-vision, big-goals, go-for-it individual is that you set your dreams and goals, work like crazy to make them happen, move mountains to get there, celebrate briefly, and then move right on to the next goal! The downside of being such a goal-driven person is that if you start to question a core goal after having worked towards it so hard and for so long, your world feels turned upside down. That is exactly what happened to me.

Having worked so long and so hard to attain this Partnership goal at a global consulting firm, I now found myself questioning if this was what I truly wanted. There were a number of influencing factors driving me to question myself. It was traumatic—that really is the best way to describe it. I spoke to a lot of people, I did a lot of soul searching, and I started to explore what life and career opportunities would look like outside of Deloitte, outside of this world that had defined me for so long. In my view and experience to date, the only definition I had of success was making Partner at a large global consulting firm. In my personal, narrow-blinkered view, anything other than that was utter, abject, dismal failure. In the big consulting firm universe that I was operating in, the general perspective was that those that made Partner achieved ultimate success; those who didn't or those who left (by choice or otherwise) were viewed as achieving lesser degrees of success or potentially even as failing, with those lesser degrees of failure varying by the path you ended up on, either inside or outside the consulting universe.

All of a sudden I was challenging the definitions of success and failure that I had subscribed to for so long. I had to figure out if I was being true to myself or if I was betraying myself, if I was betraying others in terms of their support of me to date through my career, if that even mattered if at the end of it all I wasn't realizing my full potential, and if I was just pursuing Partnership for the sake of the goal itself because it had been my goal for so long. While I loved the work and the people at Deloitte, I had significant concerns about a number of factors that were becoming increasingly important to me: the ability to diversify and reinvent myself frequently and rapidly; the ability to rekindle my creative, innovative, and entrepreneurial spirit and drive that I had always believed would fuel me to do big and exciting things; my ability to realize my full potential; some level of frustration with gender dynamics that still existed more than one would have hoped in a firm that was certainly doing a lot of great things for its women; and my desire to improve my work-life integration. I realized it was a case of "be brave now or not at all"— take the risk now to really chart my own course or continue to have a journey mapped more by others than myself. It was time to embrace my own definition of success and failure and not anybody else's. It was time to rescue myself and to celebrate myself by taking a huge risk. So I left. It was incredibly tough. It was extremely risky. But it was the right decision.

I will be honest with you. It took me a long time to get comfortable with my new life and my new choices. It took me years to relinquish the hold that my old universe's definitions of success and failure had on me and instead embrace my own definitions. I love every moment of the things I am doing and the risks I am taking. Yet many times I have questioned if I am a success or a failure. The crazy thing is that by anyone else's measure there is no question that I am being successful with the risks I am taking. I've launched and am growing two companies, I have great clients, I've reinvented myself into totally new areas of expertise, I am creating and bringing to the marketplace bold new ideas and programs that have not existed before, and those programs are getting great traction and growing. I am building a network the depth and breadth of which surpasses anything I have had to date, I am getting booked for speaking engagements, I have been signed by a publisher for this book, and I have full control over my work-life integration. The list goes on. None of these things are failures; they are successes by anyone's measure. If I saw anyone else accomplishing these things, I would gush about how successful they are. But I had to get to the point where I could understand and accept why they encapsulate success for me. It took me years to internalize that for me, success is about taking risks so I can realize the full extent of my true potential. For me success is about innovating and breaking new ground to do things no one else is doing, positively impacting women and organizations in ways that changes the pace of women's career advancement, and building a sustainable business model to let me do these things for a long time. It's about working with amazing clients and continuing to build an incredible network. It's about having more time to focus on giving back to my community and to teach my group cycle classes, and spending more nights curled up in bed with my husband and my two cats than alone in another hotel room in another city. It took me years to be able to celebrate myself, my successes, and my ability to rescue myself as I continue on in my risk taking.

Here are three of my wishes for all of you reading this book. Wish number one: that you will define success and failure for yourself and not fall prey to other people's definitions. Wish number two: that you will continue to take calculated risks throughout your career and that you will use everything you have learned in this book to aid you in being more successful with your risk taking. Wish number three: that as you continue to risk, you will experience the joy of both rescuing yourself and celebrating yourself.

Chapter 13 Notes

1   Gino, Francesca, and Pisano, Gary P. "Why Leaders Don't Learn From Success" *Harvard Business Review* (April 2011, reprint): 1–8.

PART THREE:

"Ready, Set...RISK!"

Chapter 14: A Framework for Your Individual Roadmap

In Part One we laid the foundation to increase the extent and frequency of our calculated risk taking during the course of our careers. In Part Two we worked our way through a number of specific strategies and tactics. Now it's time for you to move forward with your risk taking in your own career and apply everything you have learned. I encourage you to do so thoughtfully and with a master plan in mind. Build a roadmap for your calculated risk taking in your career so that you can apply what you have learned at the appropriate time and to the appropriate risk.

Here are six elements you need to weave into your individual roadmap: align with and manage to your personal vision; address your work-life integration; build and maintain your network; secure your mentors, sponsors, and personal Board of Directors; leverage cross-generational collaboration; build and manage your personal brand.

Your risk-taking roadmap will cover vast swaths of territory and time in your career. It will require constant monitoring and updating. It will get complicated at times. After all, there is a lot to think about and a lot to apply. But if you apply what you have learned throughout this book, if you weave in the six elements we discuss in this chapter, and if you treat your risk-taking journey as a roadmap to be actively planned, monitored, and managed, you are far more likely to increase your propensity for risk taking, your preparedness for risk taking, and the extent of your success with your risk taking.

Align with and manage to your personal vision.

Your risk-taking roadmap must begin with your personal vision. Be proud of your aspirations, dreams, and goals and go after them with everything you've got. Successful risk takers aren't shy about sharing those aspirations and dreams and goals with others. Sharing them and sharing the risks that you need to take to achieve them makes them real to yourself and others. People will help you hold yourself accountable with moving forward, making the appropriate decisions, and taking the necessary risks and actions to stay in alignment with your personal vision.

Francene gravitated towards this, saying, "Everybody has to have their own vision for their life. When I was twenty-one I wrote down things that I wanted to achieve. There were ten things that I needed to achieve by the time that I was thirty...Everybody has to do that self-assessment and see what they are passionate about, be hungry and learn different options that they have. Based on that, you have to develop your personal growth map, and you have to be willing to assess that periodically and make the changes you need to make. Sometimes what we think we want at twenty-one we don't want at thirty and certainly probably don't want at fifty. It is something that is ever-evolving...Then you have to check in with yourself to challenge yourself and make sure you are doing the work that needs to be done; and be kind to yourself and say to yourself it is OK if you want to change that along the way." Maureen spoke about the importance of having your plan in front of you, having the step by step of how you are going to get there, and being able to recognize when the route you are taking to get to the end goal needs to change against your baseline plan. Kim commented that for her it's about figuring out what things she needs to be doing now and what risks she needs to be taking now to incrementally move her towards where she wants to be five or ten years from now. The business case for the model of larger corporations partnering with women- and minority-owned businesses was part of her journal notes years before she even entered graduate school and was part of her thesis for every paper she wrote in all of her Change Management classes.

As you navigate your risk-taking roadmap to achieve your personal vision, it doesn't have to happen in megarisk leaps. Phase your risk taking for optimal results. Recall Katie's comments about her approach of taking smaller risks and putting herself out there while she is growing in her career. "That way when I get to places where I can take larger risks, I will be more comfortable with that. My delivery will be better when it's bigger risks if I've practiced it on smaller risks." Furthermore, don't be afraid of letting go of your current success and starting something new in order to keep moving towards your personal vision. Sue brought up the angst she faced when she took her first big career risk—leaving the successful team she had built up at one office and going to a different office to start up a whole new team. "I needed a new team of ten people. I was going to be taking on a hundred and ten new clients. It was starting all over again. There's always a risk of what's going to happen with the team that you've led, that believe in you, trust in what you do, what's going to happen with that business?...You've got to make sure that the team that you build—they've got to work with or without you. That was the first one, moving away from a team that I had built into a great office with great results and then going back into the unknown and starting all over again."

Address your work-life integration.

In order to support an ongoing commitment to increasing the extent of your risk taking during your career, you need to find a way to integrate the career and personal aspects of your life in a way that works for you. You can't make optimal decisions about your risk taking in your career if you're feeling torn apart. Work-life balance is a misnomer. It's really about work-life integration. This must be part of the risk-taking roadmap that you build for yourself. Your work-life integration needs and subsequent impact on your risk taking will be different depending on where you are in your life and your career.

Cathy had her first child while she was in the process of being admitted to the Arthur Andersen Partnership. It would have been crazy for Cathy to leave just as she achieved this major career milestone. There wasn't a flex initiative or a women's initiative at the time, but luckily for her she had a thought leader in her local office. Cathy took a risk of electing to come back to a decreased client load as a way to manage her work-life integration, deciding she would give it a shot for two years. Eighteen years later she's still navigating the roadmap of an extremely successful career. Mukta has also adjusted her risk taking in her career as her personal situation has changed over the years. When Mukta first joined BP, she and her husband were easily able to accommodate what she needed to do to take advantage of the risky but opportune roles she was offered—they were newlyweds with no children. After she had her first child she made the choice to work from home, a choice that was fully supported by BP. Mukta said, "BP supported me at the risk of trying to be a mother and an employee at the same time by allowing me to work from home...That was a risk, because everybody I spoke to said, 'You will never get anywhere in life working from home.' That's partially true. You slow down your progress. But it was a calculated risk. I was fine with doing that and having the flexibility and support from BP." Mukta has continued to achieve success at BP. She was recently presented with a new opportunity at BP that entails another location change. They are now a family of four, so there is clearly a more complex set of work-life integration choices that she has to factor in as she assesses the risks associated with such a choice at this point in her roadmap.

Leslie took a risk about ten years into her career by being one the first women at the company she was with at the time to request and secure transition into a part-time role to support the needs of her family. Seven years later, under pressure to return to full-time status but with a son that needed significant amounts of her time to help him work through some development needs, she took the risk of stopping working altogether for three years. Had she gone full-time instead of leaving, it is most likely she would have gotten a big promotion within about eighteen months. But that was not the right risk for her roadmap at that point in time as she factored in her work-life integration needs. You know the next step in her roadmap—when she did return to work, she took a job at Gallagher and has been on the move upward ever since. Leslie commented on her journey. "I would say that looking back on my own personal history, my taking risk or not taking risk has always been interwoven with my family concerns...The risk paradigm to me becomes more difficult if and when you're not solely concerned with your own individual career prospects. Were I to have remained a single woman, I would have taken different risks at different points.

But because of the decision that I made personally I felt it necessary to do a little bit of risk integration."

Cultural factors also affect the work-life integration facet of your risk-taking roadmap. Examples were raised by Sue and Annette— flexible working practices and the difference in duration of maternity leave in the United Kingdom versus the United States. Annette shared, "The support that the working families have in the UK— particularly working women—is much better than it is in the US. In the UK, flexible working practices are incredibly common. I'm a bit shocked at the maternity policies here. People literally work until the day before the baby is born, they get about eight weeks off after. I got nine months after and six weeks before. It doesn't make it easy for women to come back to work." Sue commented, "We need to make it easier for them [women] to not have the guilt that if they're coming back to work, does it mean that they're going to have to leave something behind with the family? I see women in the US coming back to work after a week. In my culture, that's just not the done thing."

Build and maintain your network.

You need your network with you every step of the way in your risk-taking roadmap. Invest in it, nurture it, and take good care of it. Pay it forward—take every opportunity you can to help others and connect others in your network. People in your network—female and male— are out there every day doing their thing, summoning up the courage to step forward and take risks of their own. Some may be less nervous than others as they do so, but all of them can do with a helping hand. Pitch in to help them with their risk taking. One day when it's your turn to take a risk, they will step forward to help you. I am always looking for ways to expand my network and help people in my network. Every single risk I have ever taken in my career has been with the support of my network. I truly appreciate that. My risk-taking roadmap wouldn't be half as much fun, and it would be a whole lot scarier, without my network.

When it comes to building your network for risk taking, go beyond the obvious. It's important to join associations and alumni groups that align with your career direction and interests, but also expose yourself to situations and people who will broaden your horizons, expand your thinking, provide you with knowledge you don't have, and provide alternative sources of inspiration as you risk. These alternative networks will also provide you the opportunity to showcase your unique skills that can be of assistance to others in their risk taking. Add people to your network who've taken risks and who are good at it, whose thought processes and decision-making processes in risky situations align with your own value system, and whose judgment you respect. Look for people who have laid a trail ahead of you on your chosen path. Surround yourself with both success and intelligent failure. Make sure your network is diverse. Include people inside and outside your organization and industry. Select some individuals that are challengers to or not necessarily fully supportive of your risk taking. Pam advocates for sometimes actively engaging the person that is the loudest naysayer in your risk taking, because if you can get them to come around, they can well end up being your biggest advocate.

Your family and friends are a crucial part of your network. When you make risky decisions, it's a lot easier to weather the tough times if you know you have the support and confidence of those closest to you. As Yanyan says, "The most important points to help me survive during the risky things is the love from family, or love from daddy, or brother, this kind of thing." Jennifer said, "You need that support to know that you feel comfortable with the situation so you can go off and take risks and be flexible and do whatever you need to do to make your dreams happen. But you also need that emotional kind of confidence support. My husband and I are very open—he's very supportive of my career. He's very confident in my abilities. He shows that." Leslie articulated it as, "Make sure that the person you pick as a life partner is as invested in your career and family as you are." Take to heart Francene's reminder. She said, "For your girlfriends you have to have those personal friends in a network that are your biggest cheerleaders and that pick you up emotionally and encourage you to keep on going even when you decide you are tired and you don't have more to give. If you do have a failure they can help you with your wounds and help you in a loving way to determine what were your lessons learned. I always say never forget your girlfriends."

The network that journeys with you through your risk-taking roadmap should include people who you can have a good laugh with. As Mukta so openly described, "I think that is really important, people you can actually laugh with. Life can be hard. Work can be hard. You can have rubbish days. But to have one person at least [that] you can just talk to and make fun of everything good, bad, and ugly in your life and know that it's not going to affect your relationship with that person is really important."

There are also certain people you pay to be part of your support network, and that's perfectly OK. That includes resources like executive coaches or career coaches when you need an external sounding board, babysitters to be available when you need to stay late for a meeting or attend a work function on the weekend, elder care resources if you have a parent that needs assistance with daily living, or even a cleaning service when you are flat out too tired and don't have enough time to clean your home.

Secure your mentors, sponsors and personal Board of Directors.

Mentors, sponsors and your personal Board of Directors are certainly part of your overall network. Sylvia Ann Hewlett's book *Forget a Mentor, Find a Sponsor*, published by the Harvard Business Review Press in 2013, is a quick, easy, and very useful read on the necessity for women to move beyond having just mentors to also having sponsors. However mentors, sponsors, and your personal Board of Directors all warrant additional dedicated attention in the context of your individual risk-taking roadmap.

In the context of your risk taking, there are some important nuances to consider with regard to securing your mentors and sponsors. When you're risking with the ideas you are putting forth and the high profile initiatives you have been asked to lead, you need backup. You want sponsors who are going to block and tackle and pound the table for you, who are going to vocalize their support for what you are proposing. You want mentors that are going to be your sounding board. In every story you've encountered in this book where a woman took a calculated career risk and stepped into a new role, she had a combination of sponsors and mentors. Connie's move from Finance to Sales, Debbie's move from Customer Service to Sales, Nancy Mueller's move from Chief Actuary to COO—these are just some examples. In many cases these relationships were established long in advance of the actual opportunity arising. You want someone who can help you listen for and vet opportunities and ensure the candidate pool is inclusive of all viable candidates—yourself included where appropriate—and who can be a role model for you.

Erin is fortunate to have this kind of a relationship with Leslie. Erin described how it helps her as she considers taking new risks in her career. "What's important to me to look for in a more senior woman is someone that has taken a similar course or someone that has taken steps to be where they are today, and every step that they've made is calculated and it's something they've worked extremely hard for. So someone who has succeeded, who understands the organization and is able to see something I can't see for myself. Sometimes it's hard to picture doing something different than what you're doing today compared to someone that's been in their career longer, that understands what's happening from a global perspective, or what the environment looks like, how things are changing." Mukta shared how she has used mentorship to prepare for her risk taking. "It's conversation, communication, asking for guidance and support. Every time I take a big risk I talk to a lot of people, trying to understand what they think of the situation, what they have done in their personal lives, to then enable me to sit down and write down the pros and cons and then take a risk or decline the risk." Mukta ensures that her mentors are varied—for example, women and men with and without families, people who are younger than she is and starting off their careers, and people who are empty nesters. She said, "That is the whole point of mentoring—to be able to see something from different perspectives [and] to then be able to make a smart decision."

When Bindu joins a new organization, she immediately seeks out people she feels she can learn from and approaches them to ask them to be a mentor to her. Melanie shared how she met some of her greatest role models and mentors in her life through her involvement with various nonprofits. Janet commented on how mentors can help you avoid crashing and burning as you take risks in your career. "That kind of dialog is so invaluable—to have mentors around you or coaches who can be your mirror, who can let you know the blind spots where you have gaps and who can coach you to act on those. Otherwise people might live with their blind spots for years and have no idea about it." Jan described what one of her mentors—Charlie Fote, CEO of First Data—taught her about taking risks as she built up PayTech. "He taught me if you don't take the risk it will never happen. If you don't step out and ask, you'll never know. If you don't pick up the phone and ask somebody, you will never get an answer...He believed in me and he would guide me. I would go to him with questions: 'Well, why is this happening? What do I do with this?' Or he would coach me before I would go into a huge meeting with a lot of men running the company."

Finally, carefully select your own personal Board of Directors—a crucial component of your risk-taking regimen. This is a group of people who you handpick, who have a holistic view of you personally and professionally, and who you ask to be your trusted advisors as you navigate your life and your career. Just as an organization leverages its Board of Directors to establish strategy and for governance and oversight, so should you leverage your personal Board of Directors in those capacities, especially as it pertains to key risky moves in the roadmap of your life and your career. The makeup of this Board may change over time, but for the most part the people who support you in this capacity are in it for the long haul with you. That's what lets them be so effective in this capacity. They know your past, they know your present, and they are working with you on an ongoing basis to build your future.

Leverage cross-generational collaboration.

There is such richness and diversity of thought from different generations. An excellent way to beef up how you prepare for and execute on your risk-taking roadmap is to leverage the power of collaborating with older and younger women and men. Millennial women are more optimistic than the Gen X and Baby Boomer women that laid the path ahead of them. Millennial women have been socialized to expect equity in contrast to Baby Boomer and Gen X women, who fought to create equity. Each generation of women brings unique assets to the table. Baby Boomer and Gen X women have years of professional expertise and institutional knowledge; they see value in being patient; they know how to use influence to drive systemic change; and their ability to see the bigger picture and their experience provides them with a distinct appreciation of the costs of women not taking more risks. On the other hand, Millennial women bring new energy and fresh perspective, an ability and willingness to vocalize their wants and needs without any reservations, a strong desire to seek out and embrace change, an innate sense of meritocracy, and they exhibit fearlessness and willingness to take more risks. Cross-generational collaboration is a great strategy for women to use so that we have both an immediate and extended support structure as we risk and as we move forward and upward in our careers. When we collaborate, we are a force to be reckoned with at all levels of the organizations in which we work.

Cross-generational collaboration opportunities start within your own family. Bindu said, "My great-grandmother—her generation had completely different challenges to fight; the workplace was very different for them. I don't think today's workplace is something my great-grandmother could help me understand. But what she had in terms of challenges and how she had courage or resilience or values, the hard work that she did, that is very useful as stories for me to know. The fact that she broke all social barriers is hugely inspiring for me when I look at my life and whatever limiting beliefs I pick up from today's world. I don't have the same social limits that she faced. But the quality of going against the norm, the quality of living your life on your own terms, is something that I learned from her. Probably getting myself educated, putting my career ahead of my family, and duties in terms of what a typical Indian woman should do, I could probably mentor my great-grandmother on these. It's not a one-way collaboration. It will have to be that generations help each other." Yanyan shared her experience in China. "I feel like my grandparents' generation, they had no choice. Since they had no choice, they didn't have to worry if they were successful or not. From the revolution period until the reformation in the 1980s, most of them started new careers without choice. They are afraid that their children will try to risk again, so they try to help their daughters or sons to avoid risk. That is [a] very common phenomenon in China. My generation, we live too comfortably. We need to try, but we dare not to try because we are afraid of disappointment from the parents."

We gain when we collaborate; we lose out when we don't. Jennifer said younger generations push her thinking; they bring different ideas on how people work, collaborate and get things done; and therefore they influence how we should think differently about the future of work and the workplace from both a physical environment and a technological point of view. She commented that younger generations tell her they value direct access to and feedback from older generations. She feels this creates balance and helps us push each other in our risk taking in healthy ways. Debbie and Jan commented on what we lose out on when we don't collaborate across the generations. Debbie said, "This younger generation that's in the workforce—they want to blaze their own trails versus follow in other's footsteps. I think that's great. They have a different way of looking at the world. But as they're blazing their own trails, I would advise them don't underestimate the value of other people's hindsight. It's the hindsight of those who have gone before you that can help you avoid the pitfalls that are going to slow you down along your own trail." Jan echoed these sentiments. "There's nothing better than listening to the advice of someone who's been through something, and have it be sound advice and give you that little edge that you might need next week for some meeting that you're in where you're in a boardroom—all men, all black suits. It's important that I do the same thing for young women that are out there."

Cross-generational collaboration for women is about making our candle burn brighter—about fueling our spirit, not squashing it. Mukta wrapped this up beautifully, saying, "As you grow, you become smarter about taking risk. You become smarter about making decisions that will affect you and those around you. When we are young we think we can all take on the world and do anything we want to. That's a great attitude to have. But not everybody gets lucky with getting away with it. Having access to someone of a slightly different generation who has been through something similar, who can guide you without taking away your spirit, that is really important. The key is not taking your spirit away. You can't be the wet blanket and say, 'Oh yeah, you can dream of having a career, but once you have kids, you will have no career left.' That's not the attitude you want. The attitude you want is, 'You know what, your career might have to take some changes and some shifts when you have children, but that's OK. You can bring it back to where you want it to be.' It's helping others to understand the pitfalls without scaring the other person so much that they will never want to jump or walk again."

Build and manage your personal brand.

You carry your personal brand with you every step of the way in your career. Every time you make a decision to take a calculated risk it impacts your personal brand. Your personal brand influences what other people see in you and what types of career risks and associated opportunities come your way. What happens as a result of your risk taking either adds to or detracts from your personal brand. When your risk taking yields an unfavorable outcome, your personal brand impacts how you come away from that situation. Building and managing your personal brand is extremely important as you journey through your risk-taking roadmap in your career.

Debbie's stories were superb examples of how her reputation preceded her: Her personal brand paved the way for the Officer's offer of a position in the network operations division, and years prior to that for the company President's request for Debbie to take over the sales organization. Cathy's personal brand made her the de facto choice for the newly created Chief People Officer position at BDO. My personal brand has positively impacted my ability to risk bringing new programs around development and advancement of women to the marketplace. Think about Mukta's earlier comments on how important it is to brand yourself in terms of who you are and what you bring to the table. When people take a risk on you, for you, or with you, it matters very much what you bring to the table. There are many aspects of your personal brand—many characteristics—that speak volumes about your likelihood of taking risks and the chances of you being successful in your risk taking.

Cathy raised the ability to be *creative,* to think outside the box and not follow the rules. You're going to have to be quick off your feet and innovative as you take your risks. People need to see you as someone who can adapt and who doesn't run out of ideas and ways to solve problems. Cathy also spoke about *building relationships.* The company you keep as you prepare for and execute on your risks speaks volumes about you, and the nature of your relationships influences the degree of trust others have in you. *Resourcefulness* is an important attribute in the brand of a risk taker. Toni spoke about reapplying what you already know, using the knowledge you have, and seeking within your network the knowledge you don't have to get the wherewithal you need. To be a successful risk taker, your personal brand needs to portray that you are *confident* in yourself, which will help others to be confident in you. Sue spoke about confidence breeding confidence, and Yanyan spoke of confidence as the willingness to try. Tony emphasized that in risk-taking roles you have to be *humble,* saying, "Risk taking helps you become more of a humble person because of the fact that failure is associated with risk taking. I believe that as a result of many of my failures and becoming more of a humble person—I have been humbled by many of those experiences—that you build a foundation." Janet spoke about your personal brand needing to blend a *reasonable mix of analysis and action,* and Jan mentioned that people need to know that once you're in the thick of the risk, you have the fortitude to *stick with it* and not give up when you encounter challenges. Bindu's comments about *ongoing investment in your education* and Nancy Sharp's comments about being a *lifelong learner* are other characteristics that add to the brand of a risk taker, because you stay current with trends, innovations, and new developments—all of which help you solve problems you encounter along the way.

Chapter 15: An Organizational Perspective
—Creating the New Normal

What moves something from invention to innovation? "Engineers say a new idea has been 'invented' when it is proven to work in the laboratory. The idea becomes an innovation only when it can be replicated reliably on a meaningful scale at practical costs," Margaret Grogan states in her book, *The Jossey-Bass Reader on Educational Leadership*, noted in Chapter 9. "In engineering, when an idea moves from an invention to an innovation, diverse component technologies come together. Emerging from isolated developments in separate fields of research, these components gradually form an 'ensemble of technologies' that are critical to each other's success...Until this ensemble forms, the idea, though possible in the laboratory, does not achieve its potential in practice."[1]

The same philosophy applies to developing an organizational culture that is conducive to women taking calculated risks in their careers more frequently and with a greater likelihood of success. Women cannot and should not be trying to do this on their own. There is much that organizations and their leadership teams can do to support women in their risk taking. When organizations take those steps and when those factors converge, they will create a transformative environment and culture that is more conducive to successful calculated risk taking for women during the course of their careers. This will become the new normal in our day-to-day business environment. For now, though, it's not, and we still have much work to do in the organizations in which all these marvelous women are building their careers. This chapter focuses on what it is that organizations and their leadership teams need to do to better support women in taking risks during their careers.

**Women in your organization are more likely to be willing to
risk, and they are more likely to be successful in their risk taking
if… they know their choices and actions are aligned with the
organization's vision and core values, and if they know the
support provided to them during their risk taking is also driven
by the organization's vision and core values.** If you want to better
support women in taking risks during their careers, you need to
incorporate it into your organizational vision and core values by either
direct or indirect association.

For Wayne, the topic of women in public accounting has always
been important. He's seen firsthand the struggles his wife—also an
Accountant—and women in his firm have faced in their careers. In his
capacity as CEO he has seen how BDO has—along with other firms in
the industry—struggled to recruit, progress, and retain women up
through the senior ranks. Over the last two years as they developed
their strategic plan they emphasized building the right culture within
the firm. They redid their mission, vision, and core values and changed
their goals so as to drive the new behaviors they wanted. They came
up with five new core values. One is embracing change, challenging
the status quo, and being forward thinking—the tagline they use is,
"Move to improve." Another new core value is "People first"—getting
to the "we" before the "me," acting as a team for the benefit of all.
Wayne said, "We have a profession where there are more women
coming in than men. We have to keep the women. Why are they
leaving before they make Partner?" Wayne advocates strongly that if
they want the women in the firm to stay, if they want the women in
the firm to feel comfortable taking calculated risks in their career in
ways that support their desire and ability to stay, then those in
leadership roles in the organization must be willing to think out of the
box and make some risky decisions and bold new moves in ways that
align with the organization's core values of "Move to improve" and
"People first."

After repeated turnover in their Chief Human Resources Officer
position Wayne settled on a new approach—establish a Chief People
Officer position and have Human Resources report up to that role. In
Wayne's mind, Cathy Moy was the perfect person for Chief People

Officer. She took it on in addition to her full-time job as Office Managing Partner in Boston. It was risky for Wayne to create the position, and it was risky for Cathy to take it, but in doing so they have been able to highlight the importance they place on people as their biggest asset. They've been able to focus time and attention on initiatives that specifically target development and retention of their women. They've shown they can walk the talk when it comes to "Move to improve" and "People first." By senior leaders in the organization taking these risks, they have created an environment where others in the organization—men and women—are more willing to take risks in their own efforts to "Move to improve" and to put "People first."

Office Managing Partners are now evaluated and held accountable on their approach to flexible work programs as part of their goals. Monthly Pulse reports take a look at each office's performance record on key metrics pertaining to progression and retention of women in the firm. They now reward people for giving work to someone else instead of hoarding it and doing it themselves. It's no longer all about having a large book of business. This has been particularly beneficial for women who could not invest time after hours on business development activities because of the personal cost of doing so. In the past those women would have been penalized in their career progression because they weren't bringing in enough new business. In the new normal at BDO, those same women can now take the calculated risk of investing their talents in project execution and delivery with positive net outcomes, since it aligns with the firm's core values. Leadership has created a culture where it's OK to have the difficult conversations around why they have some women on high-profile engagements but not on others. Board members serve as ambassadors for women in the firm, pushing the strategy of aligning women of the firm within the overall, firm-wide strategy. Strategy advisors focus on promotion readiness and high-potential women, and Partner Stewards shepherd female candidates through the Partnership admissions process. They have mentoring circles. They have a program called "Connect" that is designed at the national level but implemented at the local office level for development and networking purposes.

The result—they've seen a significant uptick in key metrics related to women staying with and progressing within BDO. Wayne commented that their staff turnover is amongst the lowest in the industry—around 15 percent compared to the industry's roughly 34 percent. They've also started to get more women to the Partner level and on the Board. Wayne said, "At the beginning we probably have more females than males that enter the firm. As you progress through ranks the gap does close, but even at the manager stage it is probably still in the range of fifty-fifty. But it plummets at the Partner level—our percentage is at 19 percent, which for the industry and for a national firm is one of the highest, which is not saying much. But if you take our Partners, say, going back about ten years, it was around 10 percent. We also have representation on our Board of Directors. It's only two [women] but it's two out of eleven. Previously it was zero. So that has changed...We are making a lot more progress. This year alone we made twenty-four new Partners—new Partners from within BDO, not lateral [outside] hires, and it was fifty-fifty." BDO is creating its new normal.

Women in your organization are more likely to be willing to risk and they are more likely to be successful in their risk taking if...they can see and hear from other women in your management and executive ranks that have risked before them and ultimately achieved success through their risk taking. Knowing how others have blazed trails inspires women to step out of their comfort zone and take calculated risks to accelerate their career progression. Access to those women, the opportunity to hear stories about their risk taking and lessons learned from both successes and intelligent failures, provides a basis for the women in your organization to formulate strategies and plans for their own risk taking.

Karen spoke about the leadership team at Zurich North America. "When you look at our leadership team, it sends a powerful unspoken message that you can succeed here...Even at the next level we have some strong women, and that reinforces what you see at the leadership level." Karen also highlighted the importance of sharing role diversification stories. "There was an article on Channel Z—our intranet—the other day on a job rotation and the success as a result of it. There were colleagues in the product underwriting organization that switched jobs for a time period. It gave both of them experience they wouldn't have had otherwise, and eventually it will broaden what they will be equipped to do going forward." Connie is pleased with the progress of diversity and inclusion in Northern Trust's Executive Leadership ranks and the Board of Directors. In late 2014 Northern Trust named its first companywide female Chief Operating Officer— the first in the history of the firm. Connie stressed that visible representation of women in key leadership roles makes it possible for other women to look around and see possibility for advancement. Tony commented, "It is really important to spotlight women and minority role models and what they have been able to accomplish within the organization. Their ability to be open and to share their stories creates a learning environment within the organization and provides some ideas on how to take risks—what has been successful risk taking and what lessons have been learned from taking risks. The risks they have taken and failed at are also great learning opportunities—how did they successfully manage through that?" These organizations are all creating their new normal.

Women in your organization are more likely to be willing to risk and they are more likely to be successful in their risk taking if...you've done a thorough job of making sure they are effectively represented in the pool of talent being considered for key opportunities. When you thoroughly, diligently, and consistently ensure the right women are in the pipeline for key opportunities, if they are ultimately selected, they and everyone else know it's credible and legitimate, and that they have the full backing of leadership to take the risk and go for it.

Pam honed in on the beginning of this process—open positions. "Senior leaders need to be conscientiously inclusive in the company's talent pool to ensure there are qualified candidates that are not overlooked in the process. I sometimes think there are people already

potentially tagged for roles. You could be missing qualified people—
including women—if the company isn't opening the roles broader in
the organization. There has to be visibility of open roles. The bigger
the organization, the harder that is. There has to be some buy-in from
the organization that critical roles or new roles are posted, because you
can't raise your hand for something if you don't know what it is." Leslie
pointed out that once candidates have been identified, senior female
leaders play an important role in ensuring that that the pool is broader
than one might originally have thought. Have they thought of
candidates that are out of the box, even if that is in itself some degree
of risk? Connie pointed out that it is also about who makes the decision
on who gets to fill the role. "If women are not invited, or asked, or
encouraged to take on certain roles that might show their ability to
manage risk or embrace risk, that is one aspect of it. Another key aspect
is who is doing the choosing and placement? Women must be at the
table to help bring in other women, that is number one." Leslie
reflected that the pace of filling roles is also important, especially when
there are only female candidates in the running for a particular role.
Under those circumstances, when there's a general slowness at filling
a role it can come across as not seeing the women candidates as strong
contenders. That might be perfectly legitimate, but dragging it out
wears the candidates down, and if they find the process to be overly
cumbersome and exhausting, they may decide not to risk again in the
future.

When a woman takes a risk by doing a special assignment, part of
the talent pool work revolves around thinking ahead as to what
happens after it is over. Nancy Mueller was instrumental in Jennifer
taking on the special assignment of Headquarters Business Lead role
for North America, so she feels a high degree of accountability in this
regard. She elaborated, "For that individual it can feel risky, because
you're leaving a job and taking on a project, a thing, an initiative. A
clear thing you've got to get done, but an unclear lifeline back, because
this thing will have to end. In the meantime life went on. What if
you're not successful?" Nancy shared that they have about twenty-five
people in Business Lead roles, and that as a senior team they've been
purposeful in the placements. "We want some of our best people to

head these things up, because they are big deals. So we are taking really good people out of a role, backfilling the role, then putting them in this position of leading this thing. As an organization we recognize the need, but we also recognize the people. What and how do we support them, because this would be really bad for the organization if they don't have a way back in." While their re-entry approach is still unproven, they do believe it is important to set the right expectations—it doesn't mean that you will get a big promotion, but you will have a meaningful role. Nancy said, "Jennifer reports to me; she is mentored by someone else as she moves along, on the radar screen, in talent discussions, something we still have to figure out. But we recognize as an organization and for the individuals it's really important that we figure this out." These organizations are all working hard to make this part of their new normal.

Women in your organization are more likely to be willing to risk and they are more likely to be successful in their risk taking if...you invest in helping to prepare them for their risk taking via professional development opportunities. These professional development opportunities are as much about the content learned as the networking relationships that result. It's hard for your women to risk if they are just heads down and getting the technical aspects of their job done. Exposure to learning and development opportunities, and the ability to converse and build relationships with others that have risked and succeeded, provides a support base for your women to make their own big, bold moves.

Sixty-two percent of employees at Zurich North America headquarters are female; countrywide over 50 percent of their employees are female. Jennifer spoke about focus on development and retention of those women being a key factor in winning the war on talent. Zurich places a lot of importance on networking—having relationships, access and visibility all over the organization, regardless of where you work and what level you are. They want those relationships to exist with internal and external resources. So they organize professional development and networking events such as training sessions, speed networking, external speakers, and book reviews and discussions. They vary topics to appeal to different generations and roles, and vary timing to account for different schedules. They continue to get feedback that facilitating those intra- and intercompany connections helps to get visibility into a whole other talent pool people wouldn't normally see. About eighteen months ago they started an advocate program that invited men and women at more senior levels to bring people to the programs and talk about the importance of advocating for women in the workplace. It's also provided them a mechanism to create additional leadership opportunities for women that take on planning and running the programs, which in turn creates visibility for those individuals across the organization for other leadership roles that need to be filled. Karen mentioned how they encourage everyone in the organization to invest a lot of due diligence in their personal development plans. By investing in all these components of networking and professional development infrastructure they have created a culture that turns some aspects of risk taking into a nonevent by making it their new normal. Like BDO, it has created an environment where people feel more comfortable having conversations about development and advancement of women in the workplace, and those conversations are happening in a more open and honest way than they would have five years ago.

Connie shared some of the new normal for professional development at Northern Trust that helps their women better prepare for risk taking. "Along with specific talent development practices, we have 'Women in Leadership' as one of our Business Resource Councils. Our 'Women in Leadership' group helped put together a process that allowed our women at the Vice-President level and above to learn core things about the business, such as understanding the financial metrics, the core products and services that we offer, and being able to tell the Northern Trust story in a way that gets you deeply embedded in who we are. This development has paved the way for mentoring relationships. On a quarterly basis we have breakfast meetings with our Executive Vice President–level women. We sit down with ten to twelve women in the business, and we have candid conversations about what it is like to work at Northern Trust as a woman, what key things we see as a firm. So there is a lot of deep and open engagement."

Mentors and sponsors need to be another part of the new normal in your organizations to better prepare and support your women in their risk taking. Be very intentional about the mentoring relationships you structure for your women and the sponsor relationships you facilitate. Make sure they come all the way from the top so that they have credibility and ability to drive real results and meaningful change. Leverage external coaches as an additional development resource. Invest in continuing education programs for all your employees. Make sure that women in your organization get the opportunity to be sponsored for executive education programs and other related programs for leaders. Don't be insular in the networking and development opportunities you provide to your women and think that keeping it all internal is sufficient. It's not. External networking and development opportunities afford different exposure, learning, and support for risk taking—different companies, different industries, different approaches, different resource pools, different successes, and different lessons learned. This is all part of the new normal.

Women in your organization are more likely to be willing to risk and they are more likely to be successful in their risk taking if...your business strategy includes having policies and programs in place that support your women in their efforts to achieve better work-life integration. Work-life integration is a more realistic conversation than work-life balance. How can women accomplish work-life balance when cultural norms and expectations pretty much everywhere still look to women to be the primary caregiver for families and shoulder the majority of home and family responsibilities? Certainly we have made enormous strides forward—in some cultures more so than in others—but we still have much work to do on this front. Hence the shift towards a more realistic philosophy of work-life integration—each woman finding the optimal way to integrate her professional work and personal life responsibilities together in a manner that works best for her. What that optimal arrangement is will change depending where she is in her career and life. Policies and programs that support your women in achieving better work-life integration will be a factor in the career risks they consider taking. Three examples are flexible working arrangements, supporting geographic transitions, and benefits.

Risk taking invariably requires flexibility and adaptability. When you have flexible work arrangements in place, you are enabling women to get done what they need to get done personally so they can in turn be flexible and accommodate the demands associated with the risk they are currently navigating. Furthermore, don't make assumptions that certain women in your organization may not be interested in opportunities where relocation is required. Instead work closely with them to ensure that all their work-life integration needs can be met so that it becomes realistic for them to avail themselves of those opportunities. Mukta and Vlada spoke about their experiences at BP.

Mukta has recently been presented with another opportunity to relocate geographically at BP. "It is very important for a company—especially for a woman—to understand that when a person moves, it is not just a person, it is a family. Whether it is a working spouse that is trailing or a spouse that stays home and looks after the kids—give them the support they need. Understand that just because I want to get the next opportunity in my career doesn't mean that I will allow my family to suffer." Mukta acknowledged that it often boils down to financial issues. She raised the example of the cost of schooling for children, comparing how she would have to pay about ten times as much in India or China to get the equivalent education for her child that she would get by sending them to a great public school in the United States. Vlada—who you probably recall moved as a single mother from Russia to the United Kingdom for an international assignment with BP—commended BP for what they do on this front. "The company cares about the major things—most of the things you need to do when you are on assignment. Starting with financials, depending on the country where you are going. Children's education—you know your child will be at an International School. You are supported in many things—in choosing and visiting the school before going, in searching for the house. There are many aspects that are taken into consideration."

Jan spoke about the employee benefits factor. PayTech is a consulting business, so employees travel. Their industry segment—

Payroll and Human Resource Information Systems—tends to have a lot of women. Jan is adamant about attracting and retaining the best in her field—female and male—in part by being creative with the benefits she offers to help employees be resilient and sustain themselves for the long haul. She stakes a claim on building an infrastructure that supports work-life integration. As we talked over lunch, Jan said, "Everyone wants that. There's not one man or woman on the planet that doesn't want that. But you have to put more behind it than just saying, "Oh I want you to have it." I pay the majority of benefit costs for all employees. That's not easy to do. Remember that my management team is between forty-five and sixty [years old], so I'm paying a lot more for insurance. I pay all their life insurance. So I try to give them that—to not worry about their benefits. I pay their cell phone coverage. I pay them all these other things that just help alleviate the difficulty of being a consultant. I pay them incentive. I pay them travel bonus. I pay them all kinds of stuff. I put a lot of money into them. I put a lot back into the company. That's how I sustain us for the long haul. By believing in them and not just saying it, because words are cheap. You've got to show them what you mean. I just recently added a lot more benefits because we're doing well...I upped their match for their 401(k). I started paying higher travel bonuses, more vacation pay. They were all pretty shocked when I put that out there. It was fun." Companies that are being inventive with their policies and programs that support better work-life integration for their women are creating the new normal.

Women in your organization are more likely to be willing to risk, and they are more likely to be successful in their risk taking if...you've established a culture where it's OK to fail, where intelligent failure is valued and not sidelined, where failing at something does not mean that person is a failure. In Chapter 13 we took a look at the joy of rescuing yourself from your own mistakes and intelligent failures and the joy of celebrating yourself and your successes. That was from an individual's point of view. There is also an organizational perspective on this. An organization that celebrates successes and also publicly values and builds future successes on what has been learned from intelligent failures has created an environment where it is OK to fail. This in turn implies it's OK to take a risk on something that might not turn out quite as planned and encourages a culture of calculated risk taking. If an organization demonstrates tolerance—within reason, of course—people will be more willing to take risks.

This point resonated deeply with Kim. She stated firmly, "Organizations that are serious about it need to give women real, bona fide stretch opportunities. You learn because you are doing. Give them the resources around it and understand and communicate that it is OK on that stretch opportunity to fail. Because it is not a stretch if you only are doing incremental steps at which you know you are guaranteed to succeed." Kim transitioned to how organizations communicate about successes and failures and the people attached to them. "If companies really want to embrace that kind of innovation, people don't get blacklisted because they tried something new. Real innovative companies applaud the try. Sometimes that's why you only get incremental change, because the message is 'try only if you have guaranteed success.' But if an organization says, 'I want big bold audacious new thoughts and models and opportunities,' then you are going to fail a lot before you get to the success." She wrapped up with a final thought—how failures are discussed and stories told and memorialized in an organization make all the difference in willingness to risk, especially for women. Erin spoke about how all this manifests itself to her. "Building that culture where you're not afraid to fail is having people around you who want to see you succeed, and who understand that you are taking a risk... It goes back to knowing that you are valued, and that if it doesn't work out, you still would have an opportunity. Just because you failed or the job didn't turn out the way you wanted or the way that leadership had hoped, you still have a role within the company, and you're not looked at any differently because of it."

Programs that provide your women—and men—opportunities to take risks in a safe environment are an excellent opportunity to cultivate the skills necessary to increase your likelihood of success with your risk taking. Tony shared some insights on what they do at Citi

Retail Services. "We have the Leadership Accelerated program, which brings together both male and female young leaders. We put them together into a working team. We throw a real business challenge at them, let them go away for two or three weeks and then come back and detail out how they would solve the challenge. Part of solving it requires them to put forth execution plans—what are the decisions they would make, how they would conquer this challenge facing the business. It gets young leaders early on in their career in what I would consider to be a safe zone—a place where even if they make a bad mistake, it's OK, because it's not going to damage the organization. The earlier you learn to take risks in a safe environment, the better the skills get honed. As you become more senior in the organization, we all know you can make some significant mistakes, and that can be very costly to the organization. So our thought is to foster that risk taking, bringing young leaders together early on, and by the way present to very senior levels in the organization—maybe five levels above them. So there is a lot of intimidation about where you are presenting the data to, but it is a great learning opportunity if you follow it all the way through." When failing at something doesn't mean you are labeled as a failure—that will be the new normal.

Women in your organization are more likely to be willing to risk, and they are more likely to be successful in their risk taking if...you value multicultural diversity and create conditions that allow employees to draw on their personal assets and perspectives and openly acknowledge their work-related but culturally based differences. Fear of being different stifles talent, and if it stifles talent, it stifles risk taking. Taking risk is about doing things differently, being out of the box, departing from the norm. It is very hard to do that if the organization culture stifles being different.

In the *Harvard Business Review* article "Fear of Being Different Stifles Talent," Kenji Yoshino and Christie Smith write about how people downplay their differences from the mainstream—a behavior sociologists call "covering." They conducted research that yielded findings showing this behavior is driven not just by self-censorship or internalized biases but also by pressure from managers; it decreases confidence and engagement; and in the opinion of the authors, it also holds women and minorities back. Sixty-one percent of the three thousand employees they surveyed across twenty large US firms said they had faced overt or implicit pressure to cover in some way. Of those who reported feeling pressure to "cover" in some form or another, 66 percent said that it significantly undermined their sense of self. They found covering to be more prevalent among traditionally underrepresented groups, including gays (83 percent), blacks (79 percent), women (66 percent), Hispanics (63 percent) and Asians (61 percent). There was also a 45 percent rate among straight white men, who reported downplaying characteristics such as age, physical disabilities, and mental health issues.[2]

How can people reach their full potential; how can they take advantage of all the opportunities to diversify their perspectives, skill sets, and experiences; how can they have the confidence to shift themselves on their own risk-taking continuums to take more risks if they have to minimize part of who they are? Organizations must continue to be more inclusive and embrace difference if they want to build a culture of calculated risk taking for all employees, especially for women and minorities. This must be the new normal.

Chapter 15 Notes

1   Grogan, Margaret, with Senge, Peter M. (contributing author). *The Jossey-Bass Reader on Educational Leadership*. Jossey-Bass, 2013: 5–6.

2   Yoshino, Kenji, and Smith, Christie. "Fear of Being Different Stifles Talent." *Harvard Business Review* (March 2014): 28.

Chapter 16: Ready, Set...RISK!

Today is the day I write the final chapter. I sit at the spot I have claimed as my "writing space." It is a small, round, glass table in an area adjacent to the kitchen. Situated by bay windows and a glass door, it affords me a view of our backyard and the conservancy area between the houses in our subdivision. On a clear day the sun comes streaming in through the windows by early afternoon. On a gloomy day the view outside is still pretty, peaceful, and inspiring. I sit here, hands poised above the keyboard, ready to write the end and wondering where to begin. Then it hits me. The place to begin the end is yesterday.

Yesterday was a beautiful mid-December day in Chicago. It was overcast and misty, with dampness in the air that felt like an invisible dusting of water on your skin, and the temperature was in the low fifties. It was a perfect day to run outside. I've been nursing a minor complaint with my left leg the past couple of months. Every time I ran—even shorter distances—I experienced significant pain. It's all my own doing, of course—a combination of overdoing it between the group cycle classes I teach and my half marathon running, and not spending sufficient additional time on other aspects of my training regimen. Following doctors orders, I had to lay off the running for a couple of months, invest in some physical therapy sessions, stretch more, strengthen my core, do additional strength training, change my running form, and slowly build up the mileage when given the green light that I could run again. Last week I was finally able to start running again. After two runs of two miles each last week on the treadmill, I felt ready for something a little longer. I love to run outside. The treadmill for me is an unfortunate necessity to be able to run through Chicago winters, on top of which running on the treadmill is not exactly conducive to you getting your best running form on. So all things considered, with the day being as beautiful as it was yesterday, I was thirsty to hit a trail in one of the local preserves.

I ran four miles yesterday. It was tough. Not from a cardiovascular fitness point of view. That part is easy, as I am both fit and strong from all the other exercise I do. It was tough because since I am working hard on running differently from how I have always done my long-distance running before, in a way it's like I am doing something for the very first time. Every stride required me to concentrate on moving my body through the motion in a new way. Each one stride felt like the work of three. The one-mile mark on this trail is shortly after you turn to the right, by a short squat tree that winter or summer is stark with its absence of any leaves. Just after the turn, the trees taper off into open prairie on either side of you. After one mile my muscles were tired in new and different ways. Two miles takes you up and around the top of the route, heading towards a large grove of trees. After two miles I was thinking that three miles had never seemed so far, but the pattern of my movements was starting to become a little more familiar. You exit out of the trees and cross over a tiny bridge shortly before you hit three miles. At the three-mile mark I was really starting to get into the groove. I still had to concentrate fiercely or I would slip back into my old habits, but the rhythm and form seemed to make a little more sense to me. I was able to glimpse a future where, with continued work, I could make this new running style comfortably and naturally mine. To make it a neat four miles, you have to overlap the end of your run with the beginning section, turn back when you hit a half mile to go and run all the way through the parking lot and almost to the door of the health club. At four miles my run for the day was complete, and I was elated. To be sure I was also hot and sweaty, and my muscles had that tired, worked-out feeling that accompanies any good exercise, but I was not in pain. I had just run four miles, and I was not in pain.

This was remarkable and exciting and a relief. I am running again, and I know I will be able to get back to my mid-distance races—10Ks and half marathons. It is a journey and will take time and hard work, but I know I can do it, and I know that I will do it. If I actually do the things I need to be doing to prepare my body appropriately, I will optimize my performance and over time get past this bothersome issue. It will indeed require me to spend more time on additional stretching and strength activities as part of my workout regimen. I will have to pay diligent attention to my form when I sit and walk and run until these new and improved techniques become second nature, and even then I will have to monitor myself to make sure I don't slip into old habits. But fundamentally I know that I have it in me, and I will ultimately successfully incorporate all of this into how I live my active life every day. I also know I will run more and with a whole lot more joy and satisfaction than what I experience now.

Your risk taking in your career is no different. It too is a journey. Your risk taking is a journey that started way back when you were young and believed in the infinite possibilities that you were capable of, when you knew no fear and would try anything that you felt like. You risked all the time without even knowing it was risking. Your risk taking is something each of you has experienced to different degrees as you have progressed in your career—some with greater appetite, some with less; some with greater success, some with more difficulty. Your risk taking is a journey we resumed together when you first picked up this book and started reading. It's going to take time and a lot of continued effort and hard work, but both you and I know that you can do it, and we know that you will do it.

This book has equipped you with what you need to do to better prepare yourself for your risk taking and the things you should be doing as part of your risk-taking journey. Combine that with your past experience and you will optimize your performance when taking calculated risks in your career. It will indeed require you to spend more time on these additional elements as part of your risk-taking regimen. You will certainly have to pay diligent attention to these new techniques until they become second nature to you, and even then you will have to monitor yourself to make sure you don't slip into old habits. But fundamentally you and I both know you have it in you, and you will ultimately successfully incorporate all of this into who you are and how you live your risk taking every day in your career. You and I know you will increase your propensity for calculated risk taking in your career, and you will do so with a whole lot more joy and satisfaction and success than what you experienced when you took risks in the past.

You are not alone in this journey. People all around you are there for you. Ask for their assistance and engage them in your risk taking. They will be there for you. Gain momentum from those that have risked before you. They want you to follow in their footsteps and also to blaze your own trails. People want you to be successful in your risk taking. They wish the best for you.

Let the first lift under your wings come from the wonderful and inspiring cast of characters that journeyed with us through this book. As you turn these last pages and say farewell to these incredible people, internalize their wishes for you. I asked each of them: "What is your wish for the next generation of women in the workforce when it comes to taking risks?" May all their wishes come true for all of you.

Jan Allen's wish for you is when the hard times hit, step back in time to when you had that "life-changing, goose-bump moment, and you just knew it was going to work," when you had the passion and stamina to endure anything. Take some time to remember how that felt and why you went there. Tell yourself again that you know you can do it. Pick yourself up and move on one step at a time.

Jon Anderson's wish is that you establish yourself as an international resource.

Peg Anderson wishes "that women's different style of taking risk is valued. I don't think it's true that women don't take risks. I think the way we do it is slightly different, and people don't see that."

Wayne Berson wishes for meaningful and sustainable change, so the next generation won't have to deal with this issue and won't have to fight the fight that so many women have to deal with right now.

Vlada Boukhareva's wish for you is to be open to the risks and opportunities that come your way, and through your own behaviors and values instill an appetite for risk in your own daughters.

Tony Castañon wishes "that they [women] approach risk taking as part of their every day mode of operations. That it is culturally inherent within the places that they work to see risk taking as a differentiator and to feel confident and comfortable to be an active participant in that process. That it is approached very much as part of what women need to do to make a difference in whatever field they choose to participate in. Today it is still a little bit of the exception. I would love to see it be more the rule."

Sue Duckett wishes for older generations of women to focus on the positives and help build up the confidence of the next generation of women.

Erin Duffy's wish ties back to her scatter plot concept—be willing to try new things, step outside the boundaries of your job description and comfort zone, start in one place and end up somewhere completely different.

Pam Durkin's wishes "that no one has to ask that question specific to women anymore—that the issue of taking risks is independent of gender."

Roger Edwards wishes for a workplace of the future that is far more representative of what the social demographics look like, and that we celebrate differences.

Diane Gillespie's wish is to see women use negative pushback and the force of those that don't deem you worthy of what you are aspiring towards as a driver to take more risks, hone your direction in your risk taking, make more out of it than anyone originally thought possible, and keep growing.

Melinda Hall wishes that as you dream big and risk flying high, you give people permission to reject you, because that is how you are going to be able to really explore doing something new and different.

Bindu Krishnan wishes that women stay in their careers, upgrade their skills and education, get more vocal about their aspirations, strive for financial independence, and don't set any limits.

Jennifer Kyung wishes for you to have equal opportunities and choices irrespective of if you are male or female.

Maureen Larson expressed three wishes for all women: getting equal compensation, women being at the table in significant numbers, and the stigma of being a thorn or having the "B" word appended to women when they advocate for themselves or other women going away.

Janet Lee wishes for confidence to be just as valid for women as it is for men, and for women to exhibit that confidence every day so as to better move forward with taking risks.

Leslie Lemenager's two wishes: First, find women that want to excel, help give them visibility, and help them execute on what they have to do today while also building their skill sets for the future to make them eligible for as many candidate pools as possible. Second, let companies do a better job of building out infrastructure for both junior and more seasoned individuals to be able to try different things within the business.

Connie Lindsey expressed three wishes for you with the same clarity and bright joy that shone from the beautiful bright yellow dress she was wearing the day I interviewed her. One, that any woman who has achieved success in any way would lift other women up with her as she climbs. Two, that women allow themselves to be role models and tell their stories in such a way that others can see the possibility and probability for their own success. Three, to have the boldness to ask, "Why not me?" To ask for more, knowing that you deserve it, because those things that make you different are what can help you achieve success.

Toni Marnul wishes that you take every opportunity you can to go global.

Karen McDonald wishes that when we look at metrics related to women progressing up the ranks, those metrics stay just as happy and healthy as metrics related to women at the entry level and junior ranks.

Cathy Moy's wish: "Have the confidence in yourself. Know how to solicit others to help you and cheer you on or respond to you or enable you or do whatever it takes to get what you need to dare. You don't need to do it alone. You need to not shy away, because others will step forward. It will be a better experience for you and you will grow, not only in your career but also as a person. You do yourself and your organization the best good if you find a way to take those risks. We have had decades of quietly shying away from embracing the opportunities—also known as the risks—in front of us. Don't step back. Figure out how to step forward."

Nancy Mueller's wish is that you figure out your own priorities and balance, and go for it regardless of what external opinion may be, because staying true to yourself is how you succeed in your risk taking.

Francene Pelmon wishes you believe you have everything inside of you that you need to achieve your dreams, and that you find people in your network to help you achieve your goals. She wishes for you the spirit of Nike: "Just do it."

Annette Reid's wish: "Don't hold back. Go with your gut instinct and think it through, but dive in."

Melanie Sabelhaus wishes for women to stay in their careers and achieve their big bold dreams. She understands that you want to be with your family, but her wish for you is that you can find a way to achieve work-life balance, because you can do it all. She also wishes for you to choose the right partner in life who will support you every step of the way.

Nancy Sharp wishes that we serve the next generation of women to be all they can be, because she sees them as the greatest generation of all time—no limits, no boundaries, optimistic, and not afraid to risk.

Debbie Storey's wish for you: "Women and people in general who are unwilling to take risks don't ever have an opportunity to eliminate the things they don't want to do. They're just settling for the things that are comfortable. I'd like to see women try things. Take those bold risks, and when it doesn't work, eliminate it from your list and keep trying other things...Through that process of risk and trial and elimination, that's how you find a life, I believe, of passion and fulfillment."

Mukta Tandon's wish focuses on further improvements to corporate policies and government regulations and laws regarding the workplace for women, all of which could make it easier for women to take risks.

Kim Waller's wish is about big organizations being more willing to take a risk and try out new configurations and approaches to connect with women- and minority-owned businesses.

Feng Yanyan's wish—particularly for the next generation of women in China—is that they dare to try, that they apply their curiosity to risk taking with a specific purpose and direction, and that they use that purpose and direction to make sure they are well

prepared and serious about it, so that when the going gets tough, they stick with it instead of constantly changing to something else.

Katie Zupancic's excitement and wish revolves around young women hearing about and seeing the risks and opportunities prior generations of women have pursued, understanding what they have learned, and applying those lessons to their own careers.

All of these wishes are being expressed to you in the language of risk. This book has schooled you in the language of risk taking in the context of your career. Your ability to speak the language of risk and be proficient in it is what empowers you to identify where you currently reside on your own risk taking continuums and why. It empowers you to understand how you can shift your position and decide where you want to shift to. It provides you confidence to draw on your courage so you can consistently make different choices and increase your propensity for calculated risk taking. It equips you with concepts and tools so you can better prepare yourself for risk taking and increase your success with your risk taking.

Speaking the language of risk means that you now enjoy the power and ability to shape your own destiny more so than ever before. You are discovering your full potential and becoming everything you can be as you now consciously choose to reframe more risks into opportunity for yourself and others and pursue them with intent, passion, and joy. A risk you would never have considered in the past is now something you are planning for. Opportunities that in the past seemed to be very risky now appear to be quite manageable. You are tolerating higher levels of risk across the board, because you now have strategies and tactics to successfully manage through those risk encounters. You are celebrating your decision to risk and realize the boundless reservoir of your infinite potential.

There is just one more wish still left for me to share with you, and that is my ultimate wish for you. To all you amazing, talented, and unstoppable women out there—yes, that's you I am talking about— my ultimate wish for you is simple! *"Ready, Set...RISK!"*

For sales, editorial information, subsidiary rights information or a
catalog, please write or
phone or email:

Brick Tower Press
Manhanset House
Dering Harbor, New York 11965-0342
Sales: 1-800-68-BRICK
Tel: 212-427-7139
www.ibooksinc.com
email: bricktower@aol.com

www.Ingram.com

Daniella T. Levitt may be reached at:
Tel: 312-466-7577
E-mail: dlevitt@ovationglobalstrategies.com
Web sites: www.daniellalevitt.com and
www.ovationglobalstrategies.com